EMPIRES OF MESOPOTAMIA

LOST CIVILIZATIONS

EMPIRES OF MESOPOTAMIA

Don Nardo

LUCENT BOOKS
P.O. BOX 289011
SAN DIEGO, CA 92198-9011

On Cover: Ninth-century B.C. *relief from the throne of King Shalmaneser III.*

Library of Congress Cataloging-in-Publication Data

Nardo, Don, 1947–
   Empires of Mesopotamia / Don Nardo.
      p. cm. — (Lost civilizations)
Includes bibliographical references and index.
   ISBN 1-56006-820-5 (lib. : alk. paper)
   1. Iraq—Civilization—To 634—Juvenile literature. [1. Iraq—Civilization—To
634.] I. Title. II. Lost civilizations (San Diego, Calif.)
   DS71 .N37 2001
   935—dc21

                                                              00-010393

Contents

FOREWORD

"What marvel is this?" asked the noted eighteenth-century German poet and philosopher, Friedrich Schiller. "O earth . . . what is your lap sending forth? Is there life in the deeps as well? A race yet unknown hiding under the lava?" The "marvel" that excited Schiller was the discovery, in the early 1700s, of two entire ancient Roman cities buried beneath over sixty feet of hardened volcanic ash and lava near the modern city of Naples, on Italy's western coast. "Ancient Pompeii is found again!" Schiller joyfully exclaimed. "And the city of Hercules rises!"

People had known about the existence of long lost civilizations before Schiller's day, of course. Stonehenge, a circle of huge, very ancient stones had stood, silent and mysterious, on a plain in Britain as long as people could remember. And the ruins of temples and other structures erected by the ancient inhabitants of Egypt, Palestine, Greece, and Rome had for untold centuries sprawled in magnificent profusion throughout the Mediterranean world. But when, why, and how were these monuments built? And what were the exact histories and beliefs of the peoples who built them? A few scattered surviving ancient literary texts had provided some partial answers to some of these questions. But not until Pompeii and Herculaneum started to emerge from the ashes did the modern world begin to study and re-construct lost civilizations in a systematic manner.

Even then, the process was at first slow and uncertain. Pompeii, a bustling, prosperous town of some twenty thousand inhabitants, and the smaller Herculaneum met their doom on August 24, A.D. 79, when the nearby volcano, Mt. Vesuvius, blew its top and literally erased them from the map. For nearly seventeen centuries, their contents, preserved in a massive cocoon of volcanic debris, rested undisturbed. Not until the early eighteenth century did people begin raising statues and other artifacts from the buried cities; and at first this was done in a haphazard, unscientific manner. The diggers, who were seeking art treasures to adorn their gardens and mansions, gave no thought to the historical value of the finds. The sad fact was that at the time no trained experts existed to dig up and study lost civilizations in a proper manner.

This unfortunate situation began to change in 1763. In that year, Johann J. Winckelmann, a German librarian fascinated by antiquities (the name then used for ancient artifacts), began to investigate Pompeii and Herculaneum. Although he made some mistakes and drew some wrong conclusions, Winckelmann laid the initial, crucial groundwork for a new science—archaeology (a term derived from two Greek words meaning "to talk about ancient things.") His book, *History of the Art of Antiquity*, became a model for the first generation of archaeologists to follow in their efforts to understand other lost civilizations. "With unerring sensitivity," noted scholar C.W. Ceram explains, "Winckelmann groped toward original insights, and expressed them with such power of language that the cultured European world was carried away by a wave of enthusiasm for the antique ideal. This . . . was of prime importance in shaping the course of archaeology in the following century. It demonstrated means of understanding ancient cultures through their artifacts."

In the two centuries that followed, archaeologists, historians, and other scholars began to piece together the remains of lost civilizations around the world. The glory that was Greece, the grandeur that was Rome, the cradles of human civilization in Egypt's Nile valley and Mesopotamia's Tigris-Euphrates valley, the colorful royal court of ancient China's Han Dynasty, the mysterious stone cities of the Maya and Aztecs in Central America—all of these

and many more were revealed in fascinating, often startling, if sometimes incomplete detail by the romantic adventure of archaeological research. This work, which continues, is vital. "Digs are in progress all over the world," says Ceram. "For we need to understand the past five thousand years in order to master the next hundred years."

Each volume in the *Lost Civilizations* series examines the history, works, everyday life, and importance of ancient cultures. The archaeological discoveries and methods used to gather this knowledge are stressed throughout. Where possible, quotes by the ancients themselves, and also by later historians, archaeologists, and other experts support and enliven the text. Primary and secondary sources are carefully documented by footnotes and each volume supplies the reader with an extensive Works Consulted list. These and other research tools, including glossaries and time lines, afford the reader a thorough understanding of how a civilization that was long lost has once more seen the light of day and begun to reveal its secrets to its captivated modern descendants.

THE CRADLE OF THE HUMAN RACE?

Vast flat plains of dry desert sands stretched from horizon to horizon before William Loftus, a young English geologist. It was the winter of 1849 and Loftus, accompanied by a few assistants and guides, had recently departed from the Iraqi city of Baghdad on the trail of buried riches. It was not gold, silver, or precious gems, however, that he sought. Instead, it was a wealth of knowledge that beckoned to him, the desire to uncover, study, and reveal to the world ancient cities that had long existed only in legend.

Like other Europeans, Loftus was well aware that the plains of central and southern Iraq encompassed the region that the ancient Greeks called Mesopotamia, meaning "the land between the rivers." These rivers are the Tigris and Euphrates, which flow southeastward across the plains and empty into the Persian Gulf. "Here from our childhood," Loftus wrote, "we have been led to regard as the cradle of the human race."[1] Indeed, many of the central crucial stories and figures of the sacred writings of the Jews, Christians, and Muslims originated in ancient Mesopotamia; these included the Garden of Eden, the great flood and Noah's ark, the city of Ur (birthplace of the patriarch Abraham), the mighty Nineveh (a capital of the reportedly warlike Assyrian kings), and the Jews' captivity in the greatest of all Mesopotamian cities—

Babylon—to name only a few. If these places could be brought to light, went the thinking of a growing number of European scholars, including Loftus, the authenticity of much of the Bible could be proven. And at the same time, the modern world might learn at last about humanity's earliest attempts at civilization.

Loftus was not the first European scholar to visit the Mesopotamian plains. In the 1600s several French, English, German, and Italian travelers had toured the region. Some had returned with stories of ancient stone tablets covered with strange writings, and all had described large mounds of sand and debris that seemed to mark the sites of ancient cities. Later, in the 1750s and 1760s, a Danish geographer named Carsten Niebuhr had explored the area hoping to identify the sites of the fabled Babylon and Nineveh. With the help of a native guide, he actually found Nineveh, which was then so covered by sand and earth that it was virtually unrecognizable as a city. Near the Tigris River, Niebuhr later recalled,

> I was shown a village on a large hill, which is called Nunia [a garbled version of Nineveh]. . . . Another hill in this vicinity is called Kalla Nunia, or the castle of Nineveh. . . . I was also shown

the walls of Nineveh, the which I had not noticed in [first] passing through [the area], thinking them a line of hills. I sketched a plan of all these points.[2]

The efforts of Niebuhr and the other travelers and scholars who followed him into Mesopotamia in the next eighty years consisted largely of basic location, identification, and sketching. No significant excavations were done during this period, even though the sites of Babylon, Nineveh, and some other famous ancient cities had been well established. This was because the modern science of archaeology—the systematic unearthing and study of past civilizations—did not yet exist in Niebuhr's day and was still in its infancy in the first half of the nineteenth century.

Not until the 1840s did serious excavations begin in the area. Late in 1842 a French physician and diplomat, Paul-Émile Botta, began digging at Nineveh. But a year later he abandoned that site in favor of one at Khorsabad, some twelve miles to the north, where he soon uncovered the remains of the palace of Sargon II, an Assyrian king who ruled from 722 to 705 B.C. Even more spectacular were the finds excavated between 1845 and 1851 by a French-born, British-sponsored scholar named Austen Henry Layard. He brought to light two other Assyrian capitals, including Nineveh (picking up on that site where Botta had left off). Layard found and shipped to England numerous magnificent bas-reliefs and other sculptures; and his discoveries, along with others made by his generation of adventurer-scholars, revealed that several mighty and prosperous empires had once thrived in Mesopotamia.

This was the state of affairs in Iraq when Loftus, one of these adventurer-scholars, made his fateful journey southward from Baghdad.

His goal was to find something a good deal more ancient than the imperial palaces at Nineveh and Babylon. Namely, he was searching for the remnants, if any such existed, of Uruk, called Erech in Genesis (the first book of the biblical Old Testament), one of the oldest true cities ever built. Loftus believed that a site the local Arabs called Warka was the place he sought and instructed his guides to take him there. Along the way, he passed by many earthen mounds that he knew must hide the remains of other ancient cities, some of which were no doubt mentioned in the old religious texts. "I know of nothing more exciting or impressive," he recorded later,

> than the first site of one of these Chaldean [another name for Babylonian] piles, looming in solitary

The Euphrates River, seen here, flows across the Mesopotamian plain and empties into the Persian Gulf.

grandeur from the surrounding plains and marshes; especially in the hazy atmosphere of the early morning when its fairy-like effect is heightened by mirages, its forms strangely and fantastically magnified, elevating it from the ground and causing it to dance and quiver in the rarified air.[3]

Loftus's efforts were rewarded when he confirmed that the site of Warka does in fact harbor the remains of ancient Uruk. He was delighted to find that, though half buried in sand dunes, many of the city's defensive walls were still intact, rising to a height of fifty feet in some places. The excavations Loftus carried out showed that Uruk had been continuously occupied for thousands of years. Sumerians, Babylonians, Assyrians, Greeks, Persians, Parthians, and Arabs had all lived there and left behind remnants of their cultures; and the site had not been completely abandoned until the mid–first millennium A.D., a time when medieval kingdoms were emerging in Europe.

Later archaeologists, historians, and other experts subsequently built on the discoveries made by Botta, Layard, Loftus, and other pioneers of ancient Near Eastern scholarship. The strange writings seen but not understood by generations of Europeans were finally deciphered. (The study of ancient Mesopotamian languages is called Assyriology.) And this breakthrough, coupled with continuous new archaeological finds, steadily revealed large portions of the histories, social organization, arts, and daily lives of the ancient Mesopotamian peoples and their empires. Scholars found that before the rise of the great Western "classical" cultures of Greece and Rome, so devoutly revered by educated Europeans, the Eastern societies of Mesopotamia had flourished for centuries, in some cases for millennia.

Indeed, just as Loftus had speculated, the cradle of the human race appears to have been located in Mesopotamia. Among the many cultural firsts attributed to its ancient inhabitants are two inventions of monumen-

The mound containing the ancient city of Nineveh yields a collection of colossal statues during the excavations overseen by English civil servant Austen Henry Layard.

The ancient ruins of Uruk rest, silent and crumbling, in the desert of modern Iraq. One of the oldest cities on earth, it is called Erech in the Old Testament.

tal importance—the wheel and the art of writing—as well as the first works of literature, the practice of astronomy, and the first law codes. All of these early Eastern advances clearly exerted important cultural influences on the Greeks and other later Western civilizations. With the advent of the archaeological discovery of ancient Mesopotamia, noted Assyriologist A. Leo Oppenheim points out,

> a new world of undreamt-of complexity and appeal emerged, and the historic vista of man and his adventures was enlarged by many centuries beyond the point reached by the Old Testament and classical sources. . . . Western man could suddenly perceive himself, his own civilization, and the civilizations around him. In fact, West-

ern man became then and there, and for the first time, willing and able to appreciate and to evaluate with objectivity his own civilization, to correlate other civilizations, and to strive for an understanding of some over-all design and plan.[4]

In ages long past, these preclassical Mesopotamian cities and empires were part of a living, breathing civilization, one of the most pivotal in world history. Now that civilization is dead, much of it still buried beneath the silent, shifting desert sands. The following story—of how Mesopotamia came to be, long prospered, eventually declined and fell, and was eventually rediscovered by modern scholars—ranks among the most important and fascinating tales ever told.

CHAPTER ONE

MESOPOTAMIA'S EARLY PEOPLES AND FIRST CITIES

The archaeological discovery of the ancient Mesopotamian cities and empires began in earnest with the excavations of Nineveh and Nimrud by Austen Henry Layard in the late 1840s. These, he found, had been important capitals of the Assyrian Empire, which had ruled much of the Near East with a heavy hand in the second and first millennia B.C. Before Layard's time, scholars knew very little about the Assyrians and the other peoples and empires that had existed in Mesopotamia over the centuries. For the most part, the Sumerians, Babylonians, and Kassites, the cities of Ur, Eridu, and Assur, and mighty rulers like Sargon, Nebuchadrezzar, and Assurbanipal were little more than intriguing names in old books and stories.

Not surprisingly, therefore, Layard captured the imagination of millions of people around the world when he began to show that these legendary peoples, places, and rulers had been quite real. Adding to the excitement was the dramatic and spectacular nature of the evidence Layard unearthed. Only hours after starting to dig at Nimrud (about thirty miles southeast of Nineveh) in November 1845, the twenty-eight-year-old English civil servant and the six workmen he had hired from a local

Arab chieftain discovered rooms from two separate palaces. And to their delight, they found that these chambers were decorated with magnificent sculptured wall reliefs. Layard later described one of the vivid battle scenes depicted:

> Two chariots, drawn by horses . . . were each occupied by a group of three warriors; the principal person in both groups was beardless. . . . He was clothed in a complete suit of mail, and wore a pointed helmet on his head. . . . The left hand . . . grasped a bow at full stretch; whilst the right . . . held an arrow ready to be discharged. A second warrior with reins and whip urged to the utmost of their speed three horses, who were galloping over the plain. A third [figure], without helmet, and with flowing hair and beard, held a shield for the defense of the principal figure. Under the horses' feet . . . were the conquered, wounded by the arrows of the conquerors.[5]

As more buildings at Nimrud, Nineveh, Babylon, Uruk, Ur, and other Mesopotamian sites came to light, Layard and his successors found thousands of similar sculptures. They also uncovered many tablets bearing ancient writings, as well as tombs, chariots, weapons, tools, jewelry, pottery, and other artifacts. Thanks to these discoveries, by the early twentieth century scholars had managed to piece together a rough outline of Mesopotamia's history and succession of cultures. Before there were great empires, they found, there were cities; these cities had themselves developed from simple villages; and all, from the very beginning, had been shaped and influenced by the region's unique physical and environmental setting.

A Fertile and Inviting Region

Lying roughly at the center of the Near East, the plains of Mesopotamia constituted one of the great crossroads of the ancient world. Seen on a map or in a photo taken from high above, the area's boundaries remain distinct; the Arabian Desert and Persian Gulf border the southern rim of the Tigris-Euphrates plains; the fertile Mediterranean coasts of Palestine and Syria lie to the west; the Black Sea, mountainous Armenia, and the Caspian Sea sprawl to the north; and the rugged highlands of the Zagros Mountains and the Iranian plateau rise in the east. The lowlands, rolling hills, and valleys

This detail from one of the many reliefs discovered in the palace of King Assurbanipal II at Nimrud shows an Assyrian warrior slaying an enemy.

This modern farmer works an arid patch of land in a region that was once highly fertile.

enclosed by these natural barriers featured many local regions that were very hospitable to settlement and the growth of large local populations. According to A. Leo Oppenheim:

Along the rivers we find fertile, oasis-like stretches such as those that appear here and there on the Tigris [River] and its tributaries, and especially on the Euphrates [River], wherever the formation of the river banks makes agriculture by irrigation possible. The flatlands and the narrow valleys, between the parallel chains of hills which ascend in ever higher ranges from the piedmont plains along the Tigris to the alpine tops of the Zagros Mountains, enjoy sufficient rainfall to assure annual cereal crops and to produce an abundance of fruit trees. In the plain between and beyond the two great rivers are widely scattered areas where

the local topography and the nature of the soil allow man . . . to raise cereals, although the crops vary considerably in yield and quality with the amount of rain and the care given the fields. Large tracts of land between the sown fields and the barren desert offer grazing grounds for flocks of sheep and goats, even for cattle, depending on the season and the region.[6]

It is important to point out that very little of early Mesopotamia was made up of desert wastelands, as so much of the area is today. Large tracts of the alluvial river plains and the uplands surrounding them were for a long time fertile. And those areas that were artificially irrigated were unusually productive. The extensive deserts evident in central and southern Iraq today are the result of many centuries of mismanaged irrigation, soil exhaustion, deforestation of the hillsides, destruction of ground cover by herds of goats, shifting rainfall patterns, and other similar factors.

Therefore, the first humans who entered Mesopotamia about seven thousand years ago found it an extremely varied, fertile, and quite attractive and inviting region. Eventually, they would create the world's first large-scale cities, having streets, huge brick buildings, and miles-long defensive walls. However, for several millennia these settlers occupied much smaller and simpler settlements that closely resembled the mud-brick villages that still dotted the region in the twentieth century. Not far to the northwest of the Persian Gulf, Michael Wood points out,

is a village abandoned in the 1960s when its canal dried up. It had a population of 200, who lived in mud and reed huts. Each family group had an enclosure wall of sun-dried mud protecting their house, a sleeping platform, corral, grain silo, and bread oven. The village still had an old female traditional religious specialist who composed verses, incantations, and spells, and acted as midwife. . . . So even today in the southern plain the visitor can find clues to the different lives lived by prehistoric societies on the threshold of the city age.[7]

By comparing modern villages to the remnants of ancient ones in this manner, archaeologists are better able to reconstruct how the older ones looked and functioned.

Settlements of the Fertile Crescent

For a long time, historians thought that the first such primitive settlements in the Near East appeared on Mesopotamia's great river plains, especially in the southeast, a region that came to be called Sumer. It is now clear, however, that this assumption was wrong and that the Near East's initial inhabited zone ran

through the wide belt of foothills surrounding the Mesopotamian plains; this belt, often referred to as the Fertile Crescent, stretched in an arc from Palestine northward through Syria and eastern Anatolia (or Asia Minor, present-day Turkey), eastward across northern Iraq, and into the Plateau of Iran. Only later, after village life had become complex and fairly sophisticated, did some of the inhabitants of this region begin to migrate southward into Mesopotamia.

The growth of these early settlements in the Fertile Crescent apparently coincided with (or was made possible by) the development of agriculture, perhaps as early as 9000 or 10,000 B.C. The inhabitants of the region, comments University of Oklahoma scholar Daniel C. Snell,

learned that after a few years grains increased in size when human beings planted, tended, and harvested them. Animals too changed some of their characteristics when they were domesticated, and both animals and plants were more convenient for people and

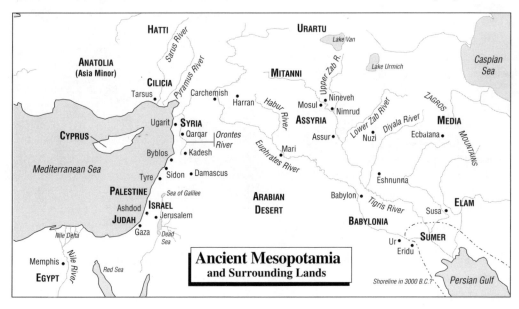

Ancient Mesopotamia
and Surrounding Lands

Shown here are parts of the moat and fortified defensive wall of Jericho, a Palestinian town that began to prosper in the eighth millennium B.C.

more reliable than they had been before people were planting and managing them.[8]

Simply put, agriculture and herding provided more food, which in turn stimulated population growth and increased the size and complexity of human settlements.

By the eighth millennium B.C., some of these settlements had begun to protect themselves with defensive walls of brick and stone. The most famous early example is the town of Jericho, in the Jordan valley in Palestine, featuring stone defenses enclosing an area of eleven acres. A larger fortified village, covering some thirty-two acres, flourished in the seventh and sixth millennia B.C. at Çatal Hüyük in southeastern Anatolia. (In fact, Çatal Hüyük is the largest neolithic site in the Near East. Archaeologists define neolithic cultures as those that practiced agriculture but still used stone, rather than metal, implements.) The town's "square, flat-roofed houses," writes noted archaeologist Dr. Trevor Watkins,

were built side by side like a pile of children's building blocks, pushed together. Access to each house was by means of a door at roof-level, from which a steep ladder led down into the living area. Circulation [movement] around the settlement was across the flat roofs. The edge of such a settlement would have presented a solid, blank wall to any intruder or attacker. Once the ladders . . . were drawn up, the settlement would have been impregnable.[9]

Çatal Hüyük's military defenses were likely designed to keep out local bands of marauders; however, they foreshadowed the large-scale international warfare that characterized the area later, especially in the second millennium B.C. when it was part of the Hittite Empire, which vied for dominance with the Mesopotamian empires.

Unfortunately, the social and political organization of early Near Eastern settlements like Jericho and Çatal Hüyük remain largely uncertain. But some evidence suggests that religion played a prominent role in the life of the community. At Çatal Hüyük, for example, excavators discovered the remains of small shrines dating to about 6150 B.C. Bulls, and perhaps an early form of mother goddess, were apparently worshiped at these primitive altars.

The Peopling of Mesopotamia

Eventually, probably by about 5500 B.C. or so, the population of the upland regions of the Fertile Crescent had grown great enough to stimulate expansion southward into the Tigris and Euphrates plains. "People may have perceived that their villages were getting too crowded," Snell suggests, "even if they may not have been crowded at all by later standards. And so they moved out into the forbidding frontier area, which turned out to be extremely productive agriculturally."[10]

Another, more provocative and tantalizing cause for these crucial migrations was recently proposed by a group of scholars that includes Columbia University scientists William Ryan and Walter Pitman. They point to evidence showing that before the sixth millennium B.C. the Black Sea, located to the north of the Fertile Crescent, was a large freshwater lake. Today, that sea is joined to the Aegean and Mediterranean Seas via two straits, the Bosporus and Dardenelles; but originally, the Bosporus was blocked by a huge earthen dam and the lake's level was hundreds of feet lower than that of the seas beyond. About 5600 B.C., the dam burst and mighty torrents of water rushed into the Black Sea lake, flooding its shores for many miles inland. Because the date of this catastrophic event roughly coincides with that of the initial migrations of peoples southward into Mesopotamia, Ryan and Pitman suggest that these population movements were set in motion by large numbers of refugees

fleeing their lakeside villages and farms. (They also speculate that the memory of the disaster gave rise to the legends of the great flood mentioned in several ancient Near Eastern texts, including the Old Testament.) Though this scenario remains unproven, enough circumstantial evidence exists to warrant further serious research and discussion.

Whatever the reasons for their migration onto the plains, Mesopotamia's early pioneers found that they had to adapt to a new environment. In particular, successful large-scale agriculture on the plains required considerably more work than it had in the hills. Although parts of the plains were fertile, in general the area was more arid than the hills and the immigrants had to develop techniques for large-scale irrigation. Fortunately, the Euphrates is a calm and slow-moving river that is relatively easy to divert into smaller channels; so a network of lush fields and prosperous villages rapidly grew along the riverbanks. (By contrast, the Tigris River proved harder to tame because

These Sumerian figurines of worshipers were fashioned in the fourth millennium B.C.

it is faster-moving, carries a larger volume of water, and is more susceptible to unpredictable destructive flooding than the Euphrates; these factors made the Tigris more difficult to navigate in ships and to divert for irrigation.)

The identities of the peoples who inhabited the Mesopotamian plains in the next few millennia remain unknown, in large part because they left behind few artifacts and no written records. The first important identifiable people in the area were the Sumerians, who inhabited the flatlands of southern Mesopotamia just northwest of the Persian Gulf at least by the late fourth millennium B.C. (The name Sumer comes from the later Babylonian name for southern Babylonia, the old Sumerian heartland. The Sumerians themselves called this region Kengir, meaning "civilized land.")

Exactly who the Sumerians were and where they came from is uncertain, and these questions constitute the kernel of what historians often refer to as the "Sumerian problem." Some scholars think they were the descendants of the original hill peoples who migrated onto the plains beginning in the sixth millennium; others contend that the Sumerians migrated into the Near East in the fourth millennium from the east, possibly from India. The second argument appears to be the stronger, for the Sumerian language was different than the one originally spoken in Mesopotamia. This is revealed by the fact that important place names in the area, such as Ur, Eridu, and Uruk, are not Sumerian. In fact, Sumerian is unlike any other known tongue, living or dead.[11]

It should be emphasized that the Sumerians were not a separate racial, ethnic, or social group. (And neither were the Akkadians, Babylonians, Assyrians, and other Mesopotamian peoples who succeeded them.) "Ethnic divisions played little part in major ancient Near Eastern societies," states H. W. F. Saggs, an expert on ancient languages.

> This is very clear for Mesopotamia. The third millennium B.C. knew no split on racial lines between the speakers of different languages, and no such split developed later. The cultural pres-

The Sumerian city of Uruk, some of the ruins of which are shown here, may have been the first true urban center in the Near East.

sure of Mesopotamian society ensured that although many diverse ethnic groups entered Mesopotamia, all were eventually assimilated, and none permanently stood apart.[12]

A convenient modern analogy would be that the various peoples who inhabited the cities and regions of southern Mesopotamia from about 3300 to 2200 B.C. shared a common culture called Sumerian, just as people of various races and ethnic backgrounds living in U.S. cities share a common culture called American.

The Sumerian City-States

The origins of the Sumerians aside, they, along with the ancient Egyptians in the Nile River valley, are credited with several major milestones in the development of civilization. One of the first and most crucial of these was the creation of cities and city-states. The first cities appeared in Sumer shortly before 3000 B.C. Perhaps the first full-fledged city was Eridu, then located very near the shore of the Persian Gulf (which has since that time receded about 125 miles southeastward). (Uruk, the site first excavated by William Loftus, is also a candidate for the first city. It is possible that Eridu was an older site used mainly as a ceremonial center and that Uruk was the first actual urban center supporting a large population.) The Sumerians believed that Eridu was the site of the so-called mound of creation, the original land that was thought to have risen from the sea at the beginning of time. Supposedly, this place was also the home of the first king and the first civilized arts and works, among these the Apsu, the most ancient shrine in Sumer, dwelling place of Enki, god of the primeval waters and of wisdom.

The excavation of Eridu began in 1949. Archaeologists dug below the remains of the ziggurat (a towerlike structure with brick staircases

rising on one or more sides) and discovered nineteen levels of occupation. At the lowest level, dating back to about 5000 B.C., they found a small shrine that might be the fabled Apsu. At a higher level, dated to roughly 4000 B.C., excavators found evidence for the construction of a much larger shrine, along with other large-scale public buildings (the emergence of what scholars call monumental architecture).

Other important Sumerian cities included Ur, a few miles north of Eridu; Lagash, some fifty miles to the northwest; and strung out toward the northwest Larsa, Uruk, and Nippur. These had begun as small villages, probably, like Jericho and Çatal Hüyük, covering only a few dozen acres at most. Under the Sumerians, however, their size increased manyfold. Between 3000 and 2700 B.C., for example, Uruk became a city of tens of thousands of inhabitants enclosed by a circuit wall six miles in circumference.

These early cities, like all in Mesopotamia for hundreds of years to come, were not dependent units within a larger Sumerian nation, but rather independent city-states, each in a sense a tiny national unit in its own right. In the third millennium B.C., a typical Mesopotamian city-state consisted of a densely populated central town surrounded by dependent villages and farmland. About their size and setup, Wood writes:

> A big city-state like Lagash had 36,000 male adults, Uruk perhaps the same. They were closely organized and controlled. In Nippur at a later period, there were 200 subsidiary villages in its territory, clustered around five main canals and sixty lesser ones, joined by a web of countless small irrigation ditches, all of which were subject to

rules, duties and control. . . . As for the physical make-up of the city itself . . . Uruk was one-third built up [with homes and shops], one-third gardens, [and] one-third temple property. . . . The design of houses . . . was identical to that used [in the area] up till the advent of air conditioning, with central courtyards, windcatchers, and serdabs (sunken rooms) to keep the ferocious summer heat at bay.[13]

An Incessant Contest for Supremacy

Evidence shows that the Sumerian cities periodically fought among themselves for various reasons. Often, one would amass unusual power and prestige and dominate most of the others for a generation or a century or so; then the balance of power would shift and another city-state would rise to prominence. This process, in turn, helped to accelerate the development of the institution of kingship. As explained here by Samuel N. Kramer, a noted expert on ancient Mesopotamia, the assemblies or other decision-making groups of the city-states

found it necessary to select one of their most capable and courageous citizens to lead them to victory over the enemy. And so the institution of kingship was born. At first the appointment of a "big

A FAMOUS ARCHAEOLOGICAL DISCOVERY

Some of the most important artifacts of the Sumerians and other early Mesopotamian peoples were excavated by the great historian and archaeologist Sir Charles Leonard Wooley, who began digging at Ur in 1927. One of Wooley's most famous discoveries was the so-called "Standard of Ur," described here by noted historian C. W. Ceram in Gods, Graves, and Scholars.

"Wooley dates it 3500 B.C.; this standard consists of two rectangular panels about 22 inches long by 11 inches wide, with two triangular extensions. They were probably carried in parades and processions atop a pole. They showed row upon row of tiny figures fashioned of mother-of-pearl and mussel shell, inlaid with lapis lazuli in asphalt on a wood base. . . . The standard . . . yielded Wooley an abundance of facts about Ur and its society of 5,000 years ago. There is, first, a banquet scene (giving information on dress and implements); then, servants and farmers bringing animals (showing what domestic animals were raised); a gang of prisoners; a line of warriors (with weapons and armor in use); and finally a number of chariots, proving that it was the Sumerians who, at the end of the fourth millennium B.C., introduced chariots into warfare."

Diggers excavate the ancient city of Nippur in Iraq in 1952. Like many other Sumerian towns, it was densely populated and surrounded by a defensive wall.

man"—for that is the literal meaning of *lugal*, the Sumerian word for king—was temporary and his authority limited. . . . But as one conflict bred another, the role of king lost its transitory character and became hereditary, dynastic [having family members succeed one another], and despotic [tyrannical]. Following the establishment of kingship around 3000 B.C., the story of Sumer is largely a tale of warfare as the rulers of its dozen or so city-states, which were bound only by a common language and culture, vied for mastery of the entire region. In succeeding centuries the Tigris-Euphrates plain became the scene of constant battle, a broad stage across which marched a pageant of ancient armies led by warrior-kings with exotic names. . . . Interrupting the cities' almost incessant contest for supremacy were several interludes during which all Sumer was forced to bow to foreigners, but each time foreign domination was shaken off, the rivalry between cities flared up again.[14]

Under these circumstances, it was only a matter of time before one strong ruler, from either Sumer or Mesopotamia's northern reaches, was able to conquer the entire region and create the world's first empire. The name of this remarkable individual was Sargon of Akkad.

THE GREAT AGE
OF MESOPOTAMIAN
EMPIRES

From the rise of the first Mesopotamian empire in the late third millennium B.C. to the capture of Babylon by the Persians in 539 B.C., large kingdoms and empires continuously rose, fell, ebbed, and flowed across the Tigris-Euphrates valley. The political intrigues and military confrontations of this great age of empires were similar to those in which the Sumerian city-states had engaged. But they were much larger in scope. For the first time in human history (and unfortunately not the last), imperialism, one nation's drive to dominate and control its neighbors, had come to operate on a grand scale. Fairly consistently the main players were the Assyrians, based in Mesopotamia's northern hills and plains, and the Babylonians, whose power was centered in the southeast, the former Sumerian heartland. But as the following synopsis of these empires shows, from time to time other groups and peoples entered the fray and vied for supremacy along with them.

Sargon and the Akkadian Empire

In fact, the first ruler and people to carve out an empire in the area were neither Assyrian nor Babylonian. The first great imperialist,

Sargon, who was born about 2370 B.C., was Akkadian, the name modern scholars give to the inhabitants of northern Mesopotamia before Assyria rose in the area. Racially and culturally, the Akkadians were no different than their southern neighbors, the Sumeri-

This metal head depicts the successful Akkadian conqueror Sargon the Great.

22

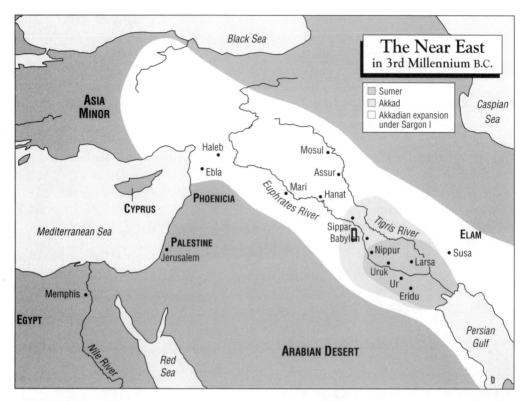

ans. The main difference between the two peoples appears to have been language; for Akkadian is a Semitic tongue very different from Sumerian. (Semitic speakers had entered the region from Syria and possibly Palestine at least as early as the fourth millennium B.C., and new waves continued to enter on an occasional basis until modern times.)

The transition from independent city-states to large nations and empires in Mesopotamia began with a series of Akkadian conquests that occurred between 2400 and 2200 B.C. Initially, a number of Akkadian rulers managed to unite the central Mesopotamian cities into a national unit. Then Sargon came on the scene. Originally a royal official under the king of Kish, a city-state located a few miles east of Babylon, he eventually established his own city, Akkad (or Agade), nearby. Not long afterward, the king of the Sumerian city of Uruk captured Kish; and Sargon promptly overthrew this intruder.

Emboldened by his victory, Sargon went on to attack and absorb all of the Sumerian city-states, his armies marching all the way to the Persian Gulf. For the first time in history, the lower and upper halves of Mesopotamia, bound before only by religious, social, and other cultural ties, were united into what was more or less a single nation. H. W. F. Saggs summarizes the effective military and political policies that made this feat possible:

Sargon was the first ruler to have a permanent professional army, and spoke of 5400 soldiers who daily took their meals in his presence. As he conquered other city-states he destroyed their walls to deprive potential rebels of strongholds. Where the *Ensi* (city-governor) was willing to transfer his allegiance, he left the old administration in office; in other cities, he filled governorships with his own townsmen. By these means he began the breakdown of the autonomy of the old city-state system, and started to move toward centralized government.[15]

Using these methods, Sargon and his immediate successors eventually expanded eastward and westward beyond the plains. They moved into Elam, in southern Iran, sacking many cities and at the same time raising the minor Elamite city of Susa to the status of a regional capital. In the west, the Sargonid dynasty conquered the large, powerful city-states of Mari, on the upper Euphrates; Ebla, in Syria, less than fifty miles from the Mediterranean coast; and may even have temporarily occupied the hills of eastern Anatolia, a hundred miles west of the northernmost section of the Euphrates.

Historians know these facts about the rise and expansion of the Sargonids' empire thanks to an unusually fortunate archaeological discovery made by the first American expedition to dig in Mesopotamia. Between 1889 and 1900 a team led by University of Pennsylvania scholar John P. Peters excavated the ancient city of Nippur (about sixty miles southeast of Babylon). Among other valuable artifacts, the diggers unearthed over thirty thousand tablets inscribed with writing, mostly in Sumerian. And some of these

contained a full account of Sargon's exploits. The most remarkable aspect of the find was that the original steles (inscribed stones) and statues onto which Sargon's scribes had carved his story had long since disappeared. But several centuries after Sargon's time, while these artifacts were still intact, a dutiful and patient Mesopotamian scholar (who remains anonymous) copied the texts onto tablets; and these rested undisturbed in the local temple for thousands of years until the archaeologists' spades brought them back into the light of day.

The Weapons That Won an Empire

The conquests of the Sargonids and the other Mesopotamian imperialists who followed them were successful in large part because they applied on a large and ambitious scale the military weapons and methods that had long been used on a small scale in Sumer and neighboring areas. Trevor Watkins here describes a Sumerian battle formation of the era of Akkad's ascendancy. (The scene he describes was carved onto the famous stone Vulture Stele, which takes its name from its depiction of enemy dead being picked at by vultures. It was discovered in the late 1870s in the ruins of ancient Lagash, in central Sumeria, by a French archaeological team headed by Ernest de Sarzec.)

> The battle-scene shows the army at the moment of victory, marching over the bodies of their defeated and slain enemies. In the upper register [band of carved figures] a troop of heavy infantry is led by the king himself; in the lower register the king is shown riding in his battle-wagon in the van [forefront] of a troop of light infantry. The

The famous Vulture Stele, seen here, depicts vultures feeding on the corpses of slain enemies. Such artifacts provide valuable evidence about ancient weapons and warfare.

light infantry wear no protective armor and carry no shields; each holds a long spear in the left hand and a battle-ax in the right. The heavy infantry is depicted schematically . . . [as] massed ranks of helmeted spearmen behind a front rank of men bearing shields. . . . What is significant is the number of spears projecting between the shields. The artist emphasizes the solidity of the formation, protected from chin to ankle by almost interlocking shields. The implied battle tactics anticipate those of the [Greek] Macedonian phalanx and the Roman legion. . . . It also suggests that the armies of those

[Mesopotamian] city-states contained a hard core of trained professional soldiery. No seasonal levy of [local farmers] could have managed such precision and solidarity and these soldiers were trained, uniformed and equipped to fight as a corps.[16]

The "battle-wagons" depicted on the stele, the precursors of war chariots, were clumsy solid-wheeled carts pulled by four donkeys or onagers (wild Asiatic asses; horses were not yet widely used in the Near East). The way these vehicles were deployed in war is uncertain. But their excessive weight and inability (or poor ability at best) to pivot would have made them relatively ineffective in pitched battle; so they were probably used as "prestige" vehicles for chauffeuring the king and his officers to and from the battlefield.

Much more effective were the standard weapons of the day—the heavy spear, used mainly for thrusting and stabbing rather than for throwing; the battle-ax, for slashing through helmets and skulls; and the dagger, used as a backup weapon. Apparently only rarely used at this time was the bow and arrow, a weapon whose effectiveness in battle would not be fully realized until centuries later. No steles have thus far been found depicting siege warfare among the Sumerians and Akkadians, but the fact that most of the Mesopotamian cities had strong defensive walls suggests that they at least occasionally underwent direct assault. Perhaps this is where bows came into play, the defenders on the walls showering arrows down on attackers.

The Rise and Fall of Ur

Sargon and his heirs must have mastered all of these weapons and methods; however, they did not have a monopoly on them. Weakened by wars with neighboring peoples who had their own strong armies (and undoubtedly by other factors unknown), shortly after 2200 B.C. the Akkadian realm suddenly collapsed. And the next century witnessed political chaos caused by ongoing struggles for control of the river plains among various peoples, including Elamites, Guti (hill people from the region north of Elam), Amorites (from western Mesopotamia), and a few surviving Sumerian cities.

Finally, in about 2100 B.C., Ur-Nammu, king of the Sumerian city of Ur, established

Ur-Nammu's huge ziggurat rises above the plain at Ur. Erected shortly after 2100 B.C., in its prime it was one of the largest and most splendid structures in the world.

a dynasty that amassed enough power to create a new empire, the second to rise in the region. Usually referred to as the Third Dynasty of Ur, this realm was somewhat smaller than that of the Sargonids; but under its rulers, prosperity, which had declined after the fall of Akkad, revived and the arts thrived. Archaeologists have excavated the huge ziggurat built in Ur by Ur-Nammu, a structure covering an area 200 by 140 feet and originally towering some 70 feet above the plain.

Unfortunately for the Ur dynasts, though, their empire did not last long. After only a century, Elamites attacked from the east and Amorites from the west, and Ur was eventually sacked, marking the end of Sumerian power in Mesopotamia. Though relatively short-lived, the empires founded by Sargon and Ur-Nammu had momentous long-term consequences, chiefly the model they set for later would-be conquerors and imperialists. Noted Near Eastern scholar Georges Roux puts it this way:

> To reconstruct the unity of Mesopotamia, to reach what we would call its natural limits, became the dream of all subsequent monarchs, and from the middle of the third millennium B.C. until the fall of Babylon in 539 B.C. the history of ancient Iraq consists of their attempts, their successes, and their failures to achieve this aim.[17]

Enter the Assyrians

Overall the most successful of all the Mesopotamian kings who followed Sargon's example were those who ruled Assyria. Among the central and northern Mesopotamian cities briefly subdued and united during the Sargonid and Ur Dynasty domination of the Tigris-Euphrates region were the towns of the Assyrian homeland. This small region, which would remain the heartland of a series of Assyrian empires for more than a millennium, was centered on the upper reaches of the Tigris, where two of that river's main tributaries, the Upper and Lower Zab Rivers, flow in from the northeast. Assur, the earliest important town, named after the local patron god, was situated on the western bank of the Tigris about twenty-five miles north of the Lower Zab. Kalhu (Nimrud), Mosul, and Ninua (later Nineveh) were located on the Tigris north of its junction with the Upper Zab. "Being a highland region," the late, great Near Eastern scholar James Henry Breasted wrote,

> Assur enjoyed a climate much more invigorating than that of the hot Babylonian plain. It had many fertile valleys winding up into the eastern and northern mountains. . . . These eastern valleys were green with rolling pastures and billowing fields of barley and wheat. Herds of cattle and flocks of sheep and goats dotted the hillsides. Donkeys served as the chief draft animals, and the horse, while not unknown, was not common in the beginning. Here flourished [Assyria's] agricultural population.[18]

Long of little political or military importance, Assyria began to carve out a niche in greater Mesopotamian affairs when it became an independent nation for the first time following the decline of Sumer and Akkad at the close of the third millennium B.C. For a little more than two centuries, a series of vigorous Assyrian rulers built religious temples and other public buildings, amassing power and prestige; and a few launched military

This is a modern archaeologist's sketch that reconstructs the original appearance of the entranceway and façade of the Assyrian palace of King Sennacherib.

campaigns into neighboring regions. Though their conquests were not on a scale as large as those of later Assyrian rulers, during what modern scholars call the Old Babylonian Period (ca. 2000–1600 B.C.), Assyrian kings built a nation and established traditions that were to last for more than a thousand years.

One of the strongest of the early Assyrian kings, Shamshi-Adad (reigned 1813–1781 B.C.), first consolidated his power and prestige in Assur by building an imposing temple to the old Sumerian god Enlil, who, he claimed, had blessed his ascension to the throne. In a surviving letter, he boasts:

Shamshi-Adad, king of the whole world, who built the temple of the god Assur . . . he whose name the gods Anum and Enlil uttered out of regard for [his] great deeds. . . . The temple of Enlil my lord, an awesome chapel, a mighty building, the seat of my lord Enlil, that stands securely built by the work of the builders, did I build in my city Assur. To the temple I gave a roof of cedar-logs. In the chambers I set up doors of cedar wood with inlays of silver and gold . . . and I sprinkled the foundation with cedar oil, oil of the best kind, honey and butter.[19]

In time, Shamshi-Adad led his troops outward in raids and expeditions, thereby expanding Assyrian territory. He conquered the small kingdom of Mari (about 140 miles southwest of Assur), which, like Assyria, had gained its independence after the decline of Sumer and Akkad. The king also attempted expansion westward and southeastward. On one expedition, he marched all the way to what is now Lebanon, on the Mediterranean coast, an area from which Assyria and other Mesopotamian states imported fine cedar wood for various construction projects. He received tribute (payment acknowledging submission) from the local princes and before leaving erected a stele commemorating his adventure: "My great name and my memorial stele I set up in the country of Laban [Lebanon], on the shore of the Great Sea."[20]

Enter the Babylonians and Others

Assyria's fortunes began to wane when Shamshi-Adad died in 1781 B.C. And it soon lost its independence, falling under the sway of various foreigners, the most important of whom were the Babylonians. Until the mid–eighteenth century B.C., Babylon had been a fairly unimportant old Sumerian town that had fallen under the control of one imperialistic power after another. About 1792 B.C., however, a new king, an extremely capable and ambitious man named Hammurabi, ascended the Babylonian throne. Almost immediately he launched a campaign of expansion, first turning northwestward and destroying Mari, then the greatest metropolis of the western Euphrates plain. Next, Assur and the other Assyrian cities fell under the

Babylonian yoke. Within a few more years, Hammurabi had become the first ruler since Sargon to achieve the glorious dream of a united Mesopotamia. The exact extent of his kingdom remains uncertain, but it likely stretched from the Persian Gulf in the southeast to the borders of Syria and the Armenian foothills in the northwest.

Under Babylonian rule, most local ruling houses became Babylonian vassals, allowed to remain in control of their own affairs as long as they did the bidding of the "Mighty King, King of Babylon, King of Sumer and Akkad, King of the Four Quarters of the World," as Hammurabi called himself. That these vassals resented having to do his bidding became devastatingly clear after his death, circa 1750 B.C. Just as Shamshi-Adad's realm had disintegrated soon after his demise, Hammurabi's empire now began to crumble in the wake of

The Babylonian king, Hammurabi, confronts the sun god in the carving on this stele.

numerous rebellions by the peoples he had conquered.

Both old and new peoples were on the move in the Near East. At the same time that Babylon was rising to power in Mesopotamia, the inhabitants of central Anatolia had established a powerful military state—Hatti, centered around the city of Hattusas near the Halys River. These so-called Hittites began raiding southward and for a short time enjoyed considerable success, their campaigns culminating in the sack of Babylon, circa 1600 B.C. Quite unexpectedly, however, the Hittites quickly withdrew back into Anatolia without consolidating their gains; and the power vacuum they left behind was just as quickly filled by other peoples. The Kassites, crude and warlike highlanders from the Zagros range, east of Mesopotamia and north of Elam, now swept onto the plain and occu-

pied Babylon. Profoundly impressed and influenced by Babylonian culture, within only two or three generations the Kassites had become completely absorbed and "Babylonianized," going so far as to give up their native language in favor of the Akkadian dialect spoken in Babylon.

The Assyrians Rise Again, and Still Again

The next large Mesopotamian empire exploded onto the scene in the fourteenth century B.C. as Assyria experienced a new burst of national energy. About 1360 B.C. the Assyrians became independent once more, and their highly aggressive kings began a great period of empire and expansion; from this time on, Assyria's foreign and military policy operated on three major fronts. The first consisted of the broad arc of foothills, ranging from the border of Hatti in the northwest, eastward

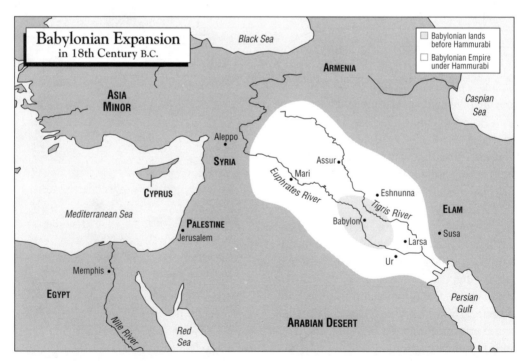

Babylonian Expansion
in 18th Century B.C.

☐ Babylonian lands before Hammurabi
☐ Babylonian Empire under Hammurabi

Black Sea

ARMENIA

ASIA MINOR

Caspian Sea

Aleppo

SYRIA

Assur

Mari

Euphrates River

CYPRUS

Eshnunna

Tigris River

ELAM

Mediterranean Sea

PALESTINE

Babylon

Susa

Jerusalem

Larsa

Ur

Memphis

EGYPT

Persian Gulf

Nile River

ARABIAN DESERT

Red Sea

This is what remains of the "gate of the king" at Hattusas, in north-central Turkey, once the main stronghold of the Hittites, who sacked Babylon circa 1600 B.C.

through Armenia to the Zagros Mountains. The Assyrians conducted frequent small-scale raids into these northern hills, taking human captives, horses, and other booty. They also built fortresses and roads with which to defend this frontier against periodic incursions by various aggressive peoples.

Assyria's second major front was the ever-changing border with Babylonia in the southeast. Numerous confrontations between the two powers culminated in the capture of Babylon by the vigorous Assyrian monarch Tukulti-Ninurta I (ca. 1244–1208 B.C.) some time early in his reign. In an inscription, he brags:

Trusting in Assur, Enlil, and Shamash, the great gods . . . who went at the head of my army, I forced Kashtilash, king of Babylonia, to give battle; I brought about the defeat of his armies . . . and captured Kashtilash, the Kassite king. His royal neck I trod on with my feet, like a footstool. Stripped and bound, before Assur my lord, I brought him. Sumer and Akkad to its farthest border, I brought under my sway.[21]

On its third major military front, the western corridor to Syria and the Mediterranean Sea, Assyria launched relentless offensives. Gaining, losing, and then regaining territory

ASSYRIA'S DEADLY CHARIOTS

One of the keys to the success of the fearsome Assyrian army was its efficient use of war chariots, as described here (from an essay published in *Warfare in the Ancient World*) by the distinguished scholar of Assyriology D. J. Wiseman.

"The principal strength of the Assyrian army lay in its chariotry. This mobile weapons-platform was in use in the area of the northern [Mesopotamian] plains during the 13th–12th centuries B.C. and then developed . . . to combine the skilled employment of horses with a specially constructed vehicle. Chariots of the 9th century were sometimes drawn by a team of four horses but their clumsiness and vulnerability led to their abandonment as war vehicles. Changes in technology enabled ironsmiths to design a light vehicle with a wooden frame set on a metal undercarriage with the wheel axis moved back from the center to the rear. The result was a highly maneuverable vehicle which required less traction effort. . . . The chariot's driver was held steady against the front screen while the rigid shaft, originally elliptical but later straight, made control of the two yoked horses easier. The car became increasingly rectangular in shape to accommodate more armor and crew. . . . On the approach to battle an additional or spare horse was hitched to the rear. The light chariot was usually manned by a crew of two, the driver and an archer or lancer, but after the 9th century a third man was added to strengthen rear defense with one or more shields. . . . Chariotry was employed either in shock action in the center of the attack, a tactic which greatly reduced the value of massed infantry in open battle, or on the wings in encircling maneuvers in concert with the cavalry."

in cycles, they at first took advantage of the fact that the Hittites and Egyptians were at each other's throats over possession of Palestine and Syria. The Assyrian king Adad-Nirari I (ca. 1305–1274 B.C.) reached Carchemish (in northeastern Syria), less than ninety miles from the sea, as did his immediate successor, Shalmaneser. These and later Assyrian conquests posed an almost constant threat, not only to major powers like Egypt and Hatti, but also to the stability of the many small kingdoms in the region, including the early Jewish states of Israel and Judah.

As it turned out, however, when the complicated balance of power in the area was suddenly overturned circa 1200 B.C., the aggressive Assyrians were not the culprits. At about that time, the northern and western parts of the Near East, as well as large areas of the Mediterranean world beyond, underwent an unexpected and catastrophic upheaval of unprecedented scope. Throughout this region almost all of the leading towns and cities were sacked, burned, and destroyed, most never to be rebuilt; among them were Hattusas and the other important Hittite centers, bringing about Hatti's sudden and utter collapse.[22]

Although Assur and the other cities of the Assyrian heartland managed to survive the catastrophe, Assyria slowly declined in power and influence over the course of the next two centuries. A strong king, Tiglathpileser I, was assassinated circa 1077 B.C., and his immediate successors, far less vigorous and capable than he, were unable to maintain the cohesion of so large a realm inhabited by so many diverse peoples. So that realm quickly shrank, shedding its conquered territories one by one until, some sixteen decades after Tiglathpileser's death, all that remained was the core—the traditional Assyrian heartland centered around Assur and Nineveh.

This did not mark the end of Assyrian imperialism, however. In the early ninth century B.C., Assyria was in a sense reborn under a series of strong kings, and the realm once more expanded to include much of the Near East. It reached its height under Sargon II (reigned 722–705 B.C.) and his immediate successors—Sennacherib, Esarhaddon, and Assurbanipal—who are collectively referred to as the Sargonids (not to be confused with the earlier Akkadian Sargonids). At one point, their holdings stretched from the Persian Gulf in the east to Egypt and Palestine in the west, constituting the largest empire the world had yet seen.

The Sargonids gained this spectacular success almost completely through naked aggression—fielding large armies and conducting large-scale, ruthless sieges of enemy towns. Archaeologists have managed to reconstruct one of their most famous sieges, of the Hebrew town of Lachish (south of Jerusalem), by Sennacherib in the early seventh century B.C. First, Austen Henry Layard found the event depicted in pictorial detail in the spectacular bas-reliefs he unearthed in that king's palace at Nineveh. The Assyrian sculptors who created these reliefs (which are now in the British Museum in London) worked from sketches made by Sennacherib's campaign artists, who watched the siege from a nearby hill. Further information about the siege came from the 1973–87 excavations at

A relief from Nineveh shows Assyrian warriors impaling Jewish prisoners after the capture of Lachish.

Lachish directed by Israeli archaeologist David Ussishkin. Biblical scholar Roberta Harris explains:

> Ussishkin's excavations uncovered the remains of the attacker's siege ramp—the only ancient Assyrian siege ramp yet discovered. It reached up the southwest angle of the city mound to the defensive wall, where huge amounts of weapons and debris have been found. . . . To Ussishkin's surprise, he also found evidence for a Judaean counter-ramp, erected within the city in haste, and probably under

fire, to give the defenders the advantage of height and to protect the walls against the onslaught of the battering rams.[23]

Despite the heroic defense attested by these finds, Lachish fell to Sennacherib.

Assyria's Enemies Close In

But though the empire acquired through such conquests was larger than ever, it was increasingly beset by both external and internal threats. In the last years of Assurbanipal's reign (668–627 B.C.) numerous rebellions, large and small, occurred; and the

This exquisite relief commissioned by King Assurbanipal shows him inspecting the war booty collected after his defeat of the Elamites (ca. 639 B.C.).

34

ASSURBANIPAL RAVAGES ELAM

These are excerpts from the surviving official account of Assurbanipal's destructive campaign into Elam (quoted from Luckenbill's *Ancient Records*), which ended with that nation's annihilation in about 639 B.C.

"The temple tower of Susa . . . I destroyed. . . . The sanctuaries of Elam I destroyed totally. Its gods and goddesses I scattered to the winds. . . . The tombs of their earlier and later kings, who did not fear Assur . . . and who had plagued the kings, my fathers, I destroyed. . . . I exposed them to the sun. Their bones I carried off to Assyria. . . . I devastated the provinces of Elam. Salt . . . I scattered over them. . . . In a month of days I ravaged Elam to its farthest border. The noise of people, the tread of cattle and sheep, the glad shouts of rejoicing, I banished from its fields. Wild asses, gazelles and all kinds of beasts of the plain, I caused to lie down among them, as if at home."

empire's stability was further weakened by civil wars and their resulting internal devastation. After Assurbanipal's death, the situation only worsened: Two of his sons fought each other for the throne, keeping the country in a state of disarray; and Assyria found itself facing steadily mounting external threats, as all over the Near East its subjects and vassals took advantage of its troubles, either severing ties with the central authority in Nineveh or simply ignoring it.

As the crisis intensified, the most potent and immediate danger to Assyria in this regard came from its longtime archenemy, Babylonia. In 626 B.C. a Babylonian public official named Nabopolassar ousted the Assyrian garrison from the capital and seized the throne. This marked the inauguration of Babylon's greatest and most famous dynasty, the Chaldean (or Neo-Babylonian), whose empire would rule lower Mesopotamia in splendor for nearly a century. Nabopolassar

had not forgotten the humiliations his ancestors had suffered in their failed attempts to liberate Babylonia from Assyrian domination. Once firmly in control in Babylon, he carried on the war, driving the Assyrians out of one Babylonian city after another. By about 616 B.C. he felt ready to move against Assyria itself, and his advance along the Euphrates was captured in a Babylonian chronicle of his reign:

In the tenth year [of his reign], Nabopolassar, in the month of *Aiaru* [April/May], mobilized the Babylonian army and marched up the bank of the Euphrates. . . . In the month of *Abu* [July/August] they reported that the Assyrian army was in the city of Kablini. Nabopolassar went up against them. . . . He made an attack upon the Assyrian army. The army of Assyria . . . sustained a decisive defeat. They took many of them prisoners . . . and [many of] the nobles of Assyria they captured.[24]

Nabopolassar also laid siege to the city of Assur, but he failed to capture it. As it turned out, it would take the rise of still another powerful empire to finish off the ailing but stubborn Assyrians.

Even as the Assyrian kings had begun to spread their harsh rule over large sections of the Near East in the ninth century B.C., the seeds of their destruction had already been planted in the uplands of the Iranian plateau. Perhaps sometime between 1100 and 1000 B.C., small groups identifying themselves as

"Aryans" descended from the steppe lands west and north of the Caspian Sea and onto the upland plateau east of the Zagros range. (The name Iran, which later came to identify the region, is derived from the word *aryanam*, meaning "land of the Aryans.") Among these peoples were the Medes, at first a loose confederation of tribes that grew more populous and powerful during the same years that the Assyrian Empire was expanding across the Near East.

By the mid–eighth century, the two peoples were already engaged in periodic wars, as recorded in the annals of the Assyrian monarchs Tiglathpileser III and Sargon II. After defeating various Median groups, As-

Median dignitaries are depicted in this Assyrian relief. The Assyrians signed treaties with the Medes, but these agreements were eventually broken as the Medes engaged in a burst of expansion.

syria signed treaties supposedly bringing them into the Assyrian realm. Despite such agreements, however, the peoples of the Iranian plateau, far from the central authority in Nineveh and difficult to police, remained largely independent of Assyrian control; and the Median chieftains continued a process already well under way, namely the unification of their respective tribes into a formidable nation.

This rise in Median unity and power culminated in the accession in 625 B.C. of Cyaxares II, a dynamic ruler who instituted a highly effective program of military expansion and reorganization. He divided his spearmen, archers, and cavalry into distinct units, each of which was trained separately and used in a specific manner on the battlefield. He also instituted standardized military uniforms, consisting of a long-sleeved leather tunic that ended above the knee, held by a double belt with a round buckle; leather trousers; laced shoes with projecting tips; and on the head a round felt cap with a neck flap.

With Babylonia revitalized and an ambitious new empire, Media, flexing its muscles, the Near East now featured three powerful rival empires. In retrospect, it is clear that all three—Assyria, Babylonia, and Media—were doomed to the same ignoble fate. As has happened repeatedly in history, the rulers and inhabitants of each likely assumed that their imperial state would remain powerful and prosperous indefinitely. No one at the time could have guessed that all three empires, despite their might and influence, would decline and collapse in considerably less than a century; or that Neo-Babylonia would prove to be the last of the long string of great empires that had originated within Mesopotamia itself.

CHAPTER THREE

HIGH CULTURE AND ART IN ANCIENT MESOPOTAMIA

Almost all large and prosperous ancient civilizations had their cultural golden ages, usually fairly brief spurts of activity in which they produced great and influential art, sculpture, architecture, literature, scientific discoveries and inventions, and/or other noteworthy creative endeavors. Ancient Greece, for instance, had its so-called Age of Pericles in the fifth century B.C., which resulted in the magnificent Parthenon temple and the immortal theatrical tragedy *Oedipus Rex.* For ancient Rome, the peak of high culture was the Augustan Age. In the late first century B.C. and early first century A.D., Roman architects erected numerous monumental structures of polished marble, and Roman writers produced some of the greatest literary works of all times, including Virgil's epic poem, *The Aeneid.*

Identifying a single such overriding, awe-inspiring golden age for ancient Mesopotamia is not so easy, however. This is because a series of great peoples and empires came and went over the course of several millennia in the region; and each made its own unique contributions to the area's ever growing and evolving cultural melting pot. Therefore, several brief flurries of exceptional creative activity might be viewed as golden ages. Singled out here are three such seminal contributions—the Sumerians' invention of writing and literature, along with their religion, which became universal in Mesopotamia; Assyria's magnificent achievements in sculpture,

This Sumerian clay tablet bears cuneiform characters recording numbers of sheep and goats.

especially bas-reliefs depicting the accomplishments of the kings; and Babylonian architecture, including the legendary Tower of Babel, the monumental walls of Babylon, as well as that city's fabled Hanging Gardens. Though Mesopotamia certainly produced other elements of high culture, these are universally acknowledged among the greatest.

The Invention of Writing

The Sumerians are credited with one of the greatest cultural advances in human history—the development of writing. Sometime between 3300 and 3000 B.C., a complex writing system appeared in Sumer, the earliest examples of which have been found in the ruins of the city of Uruk. The invention then quickly spread to other parts of the Near East and eventually beyond. The initial process was simple but ingenious. Scribes pressed pointed sticks, styluses, or other objects into moist clay tablets, and when the tablets dried and hardened, they became cumbersome but permanent records, the world's first versions of letters, account sheets, and books.

In its most mature form, this writing system consisted mainly of small wedge-shaped marks arranged in various combinations. Modern scholars dubbed it "cuneiform" after the Latin word *cuneus*, meaning wedge- or nail-shaped. There were between five hundred and six hundred separate cuneiform signs in all, requiring a great deal of time and effort to master, so it is likely that only a handful of scribes and other highly educated people could read and write. What is more, this complexity made it very difficult for modern scholars to decipher. In the following excerpt from his informative book *Civilization Before Greece and Rome*, H. W. F. Saggs briefly summarizes how they managed to solve this linguistic puzzle:

The decipherment of the wedge-shaped inscriptions set the learned world a challenge. There had been scholars working on it since the late eighteenth century. A Dane, Carsten Niebuhr, who traveled in Arabia and Persia in the 1760s, had noticed that at Persepolis in Persia [southern Iran] there were inscriptions on stone with three different forms of . . . [cuneiform] script. . . . Niebuhr observed that one of the forms . . . contained well under fifty different signs, and correctly deduced that it must be alphabetic. A young German scholar, G. F. Grotefend, worked on this script, and by 1802 . . . correctly [identified] about a third of the characters. The language was an early form of Persian. There was no significant advance upon Grotefend's partial decipherment until the 1840s, when a breakthrough was effected by . . . [English linguist] Henry Creswicke Rawlinson. . . . He spent his spare time copying inscriptions . . . in the three different scripts already mentioned . . . and in 1846 he was able to publish a paper giving a complete decipherment of the Old Persian alphabetic cuneiform. . . . But the two other scripts remained to be solved. Rawlinson recognized that one of these was obviously used for the language of Babylon, since the same system was found on the bricks from that city. We now call that language . . . Akkadian; Babylonian was one main dialect of it and Assyrian another. . . . In the long trilingual inscription, his decipherment of the Old Persian version gave him the general sense and a number of proper names.

Using this and new inscriptions . . . Rawlinson had taken major steps toward the decipherment of Akkadian cuneiform by 1849. Other scholars were working on the script, and it quickly became possible to make out the sense of long texts and to begin to recover the details of the ancient history of the two main kingdoms in the area in the first and second millennia B.C., Babylonia and Assyria.[25]

Of the thousands of cuneiform tablets discovered since the mid-1800s, the vast majority consist of dry administrative and financial records, including bills, accounts received, inventories, volumes of barley or other foodstuffs, and measures of land

English linguist Henry C. Rawlinson, who made major contributions to the decipherment of cuneiform scripts.

parcels. Though monotonous, these reveal much about social customs and economic practices, especially among members of the upper classes, who owned the land and controlled commerce.

Some Ancient Mesopotamian Wisdom

However, some of Mesopotamia's cuneiform tablets preserve actual literature. The content of this literature is quite varied, including myths about and hymns dedicated to the gods; tales of the adventures of human heroes; odes extolling the deeds and virtues of kings; lamentations for the fall of cities and rulers; poems that were sung at weddings and perhaps other important social gatherings; and proverbs and wise sayings.

The latter category, generally referred to as "wisdom literature," was one of the most popular of all. Some of the simpler but highly witty or practical sayings that have survived include: "If you take the field of an enemy, the enemy will come and take your field"; "For a man's pleasure there is marriage; on thinking it over, there is divorce"; and "In a city that has no watch dogs, the fox is the overseer."[26] The following longer example, "The Poem of the Righteous Sufferer," is spoken by a man who has supposedly been forsaken by the gods and whose tone is therefore bitter and sarcastic:

Who came to life yesterday, died today.
In but a moment man is cast into
gloom, suddenly crushed,
One moment he will sing for joy,
And in an instant he will wail—a
mourner,
Between morning and nightfall men's
mood may change:

When they are hungry they become
　like corpses,
When they are full they will rival their
　god,
When things go well they will prate
　[chatter] of rising up to heaven.
And when in trouble, [they will] rant
　about descending into hell.[27]

The Epic Tale of Gilgamesh

Perhaps the most important examples of
Sumerian literature were the creation myths.
These not only became the common her-
itage of all later Mesopotamian cultures, but
went on to influence several neighboring
peoples, among them the Hebrews, who
passed them along in their own literature
(including the Old Testament). The most famous and influential of these myths appears
in the *Epic of Gilgamesh*. This large compila-
tion of early heroic tales and folklore was
first collected into a unified whole circa
2000 B.C. by an unknown Babylonian scribe.
(Although written in Akkadian, rather than
Sumerian, the themes, style, and names of
the characters and places are Sumerian,
showing that most of the content dates from
Sumerian times.) The story centers on the
exploits of the title character. Gilgamesh was
probably originally a real Sumerian ruler,
possibly the king of Uruk, as one legend
states. No specific evidence of his rule has
been found, but, as Daniel Snell points out,
"the problem of finding the historical Gilgamesh is complicated by the fact that the
name Gilgamesh is almost certainly a later
epithet for the hero, not the name he bore in
life; it may mean 'heroic ancestor.'"[28]

The *Epic of Gilgamesh* was first translated
in 1872 by English scholar and archaeologist
George Smith. Of the work's approximately
thirty-five hundred lines, about fifteen re-

*This is a modern sketch of a stone relief depicting
the Sumerian hero Gilgamesh.*

mained missing at the time of the translation. Both scholars and the educated community considered the epic so important
that a newspaper, the *Daily Telegraph*, fi-
nanced an expedition to Iraq to find the
missing lines. In an extraordinary turn of
good fortune, the team, led by Smith himself, achieved its goal in the first few weeks
of digging. In his *Assyrian Discoveries*, published in 1875, Smith wrote:

> On the 14th of May . . . I sat down to
> examine the store of fragments of
> cuneiform inscriptions from the day's
> digging, taking out and brushing off
> the earth from the fragments to read

their contents. On cleaning one of them I found to my surprise and gratification that it contained the greater portion of seventeen lines of inscription belonging to the first column of the Chaldean [Babylonian] account of the Deluge [great flood], and fitting into the only place where there was a serious blank in the story. When I had first published the account of this tablet I had conjectured that there were about fifteen lines wanting [lacking] in this part of the story, and now with this portion I was enabled to make it nearly complete.[29]

In the epic, Gilgamesh searches long and hard for the secret of eternal life, only to find in the end that no human being can escape old age and death. Along the way he has many adventures, including a meeting with Utnapishtim (whom the Sumerians called Ziusudra), who tells him the story of the great flood, an attempt by the gods to "destroy the seed of humanity." Warned of the impending deluge by the god Ea, Utnapishtim builds a great ark. "All that I had I loaded onto her," he recalls. "All that I had of living beings of all kinds I loaded on her. I brought to the ship all my family and household; cattle . . . [and] beasts of the field, all the workmen I brought on board." Then the flood strikes, destroying humanity and leaving the landscape "level as a flat roof." Finally, the ark comes to rest on a mountaintop protruding from the floodwaters.

When the seventh day arrived, I sent forth a dove, letting it free. . . . Not finding a resting place, it came back. I sent forth a swallow. . . . Not finding a resting place, it came back. I sent forth a raven. . . . The raven went and saw the decrease of the waters. It ate, croaked, but did not turn back. Then I let all [on board the ark] out to the four regions [of the earth, i.e., the Near East, then the known world] and brought an offering [sacrifice to the gods].[30]

As is well known, more than a thousand years later, the Hebrew scribes who compiled the books of the biblical Old Testament included their own version of this flood tale, changing the name of the ark's builder to Noah. Other elements and motifs of the Gilgamesh story later filtered out of the Near East, cropping up in the Greek Homeric epics—the *Iliad* and *Odyssey*—and, with Islamic colorings, in the Arabic *Thousand and One Nights*.

The dove has been released from the great ark by Noah (the Hebrew version of Utnapishtim).

A SUMERIAN HYMN

This Sumerian poem (quoted from Jean Bottéro's *Mesopotamia: Writing, Reasoning, and the Gods*), which was written in the mid– to late third millennium B.C., is a hymn of praise to the god Enlil, the sovereign deity of the universe.

"Enlil! his authority is far-reaching, his word is sublime and holy.

His decisions are unalterable, he decides fates forever!

His eyes scrutinize the entire world!

When the honorable Enlil sits down in majesty on his sacred and sublime throne,

When he exercises with perfection his power as Lord and King,

Spontaneously the other gods prostrate [lie flat on their faces] before him and obey his orders without protest!

He is the great and powerful ruler who dominates Heaven and Earth,

Who knows all and understands all!"

Survivals of Language and Religion

Like its cuneiform writing and wide-ranging literature, Sumer's language and religion survived its political decline in the late third millennium B.C. After 2000 B.C. the Sumerian language was no longer widely spoken, as dialects of Akkadian, including an early form of Babylonian, came into general use in both northern and southern Mesopotamia. However, Sumerian remained a sort of sacred and literary language utilized by priests and scholars, just as Latin was (and still is) used by churchmen and scholars after it was no longer spoken. Meanwhile, the Akkadian speakers whose dialects became dominant in the region adopted the Sumerians' cuneiform writing system to their own tongue. This shows that system's tremendous flexibility, since the two languages are as different from each other as Latin is from Chinese. At the same time, the survival of Sumerian religion provided a basic model that other peoples of the Near East followed long after the Sumerians themselves had disappeared. "For more than three-thousand years," writes Georges Roux,

the religious ideas promoted by the Sumerians played an extraordinary part in the public and private life of the Mesopotamians, modeling their institutions, coloring their works of art and literature, pervading every form of activity from the highest functions of the kings to the day-to-day occupations of their subjects. . . . The fact that Sumerian society crystallized

The sun god Shamash (or Utu in the Sumerian pantheon) receives homage from three human suppliants in this relief on a ninth-century B.C. *Babylonian tablet.*

around temples . . . had deep and lasting consequences. In theory, for instance, the land never ceased to belong to the gods, and the mighty Assyrian monarchs whose empire extended from the Nile to the Caspian Sea [in the early seventh century B.C.] were the humble servants of their god Assur, just as the governors of Lagash, who ruled over a few square miles of Sumer, were those of their god Ningersu.[31]

The most revered of the Sumerian gods were An (or Anu, whose main temple was in Uruk), sovereign of the universe; Enlil (his worship centered in Nippur), creator and ruler of earth; Enki, god of the waters; and Enzu, Utu, and Inanna (or Ninni), deities of the moon, sun, and planet Venus respectively. The Babylonians, Assyrians, and other peoples who succeeded the Sumerians in the region and adopted their culture also borrowed these gods, sometimes changing their names. Thus, Enki became Ea, Enzu became Sin, Utu became Shamash, and Inanna became Ishtar in later Mesopotamian pantheons (groups of gods). At the same time, the Babylonians identified their chief god Marduk and the Assyrians their god Assur with the Sumerian Enlil. These gods, like those of the later Greeks and Romans, were seen as having human form as well as human qualities, frailties, and passions. "In brief," says Roux, "they represented the best and worst of human nature on a superhuman scale."[32]

Assyria's Exquisite Bas-Reliefs and Other Arts

Though Assyria, as one of Sumer's chief heirs, relied to a great extent on Sumerian cultural models, the Assyrians made some important cultural contributions of their own, particularly in the arts. Of those Assyrian arts that survive, without doubt the most striking and original were the magnificent carved stone bas-reliefs that adorned the walls of the royal palaces. Especially numerous and striking were those created in the reigns of the Sargonids, making the seventh century B.C. a golden age of wall sculpture. In room after room, corridor after corridor, many thousands of feet of reliefs bore detailed scenes of the lives and exploits of the reigning monarchs. In some, they can be seen dining in picturesque gardens laden with fruit trees; in others, they hunt lions or receive tribute from vassals; and in still others, they lead their armies in battle. About the exquisite quality of these works, the late, noted historian Chester G. Starr remarked:

> From the artistic point of view Assyrian relief was the highest point thus far reached in Near Eastern art. Sieges and battles at times had almost a sense of space, and in the scenes of hunting, animals were shown with more realism than had ever before been achieved. Here the artists gave a vivid sense of motion, even at times of pity for the dying lions or wild asses; in other scenes the king, with

fringed robe, long curled beard, and heavy shoulders and legs, was a static but powerful figure. Not until we come to Roman imperial art shall we find again artists who concentrated upon seizing the specific quality of individual historical events.[33]

Nowhere in ancient Assyria was the artistic depiction of historical events more vivid than in Sennacherib's palace at Nineveh. Here, Austen Henry Layard excavated hundreds of feet of exquisite reliefs showing that king fighting his enemies, marching in his victory parade, feasting in his palace, and so forth. The various events and scenes are depicted in a formal, sometimes exaggerated manner, as one would expect from works meant to be a combination of art and propaganda; yet the artists went to great pains to capture the court customs, costumes, architecture, social rankings,

This depiction of King Sennacherib illustrates the remarkable level of detail in many Assyrian reliefs.

weapons, military tactics, religious rituals, musical instruments, and other aspects of real life in stunning detail. In his fascinating record of his discoveries in this archaeological treasure trove—*Nineveh and Its Remains*, first published in 1867—Layard provides this vivid description of some of these reliefs:

> The sculptures . . . represented the wars of the king, and his victories over foreign nations. The upper bas-reliefs . . . formed one subject—the king, with his warriors, in battle under the walls of a hostile castle. He stood, gorgeously attired, in a chariot drawn by three horses, richly caparisoned [outfitted with decorative bridles, saddles, and other trappings], and was discharging an arrow either against those who defended the walls; or against a warrior, who, already wounded, was falling from his chariot. An attendant protected the person of the king with a shield, and a charioteer held the reins, and urged on the horses. . . . In each Assyrian chariot was a standard [symbol of a military unit]—the devices which were enclosed in a circle ornamented with tassels and streamers, being an archer . . . standing on a bull. . . . At the bottom of the first bas-relief were wavy lines, to indicate water or a river, and trees were scattered over both. . . . On the upper part of the two

ASSURNASIRPAL BUILDS A NEW PALACE

Along with their relief sculptures, the ancient Assyrians produced some noteworthy examples of architecture, in particular some imposing palaces. The last major Sargonid ruler, Assurnasirpal, built one of these palaces when he renovated the city of Nimrud, as described in this excerpt from his annals (quoted in Luckenbill's *Ancient Records*).

"That city had fallen into ruins and lay prostrate. That city I built anew, and the peoples whom my hand had conquered, from the lands which I brought under my sway . . . I took and I settled them therein. The ancient mound I destroyed, and I dug down to the water level. . . . A palace of cedar, cypress, juniper, boxwood, mulberry, pistachio-wood, and tamarisk, for my royal dwelling and for my lordly pleasure for all time I founded therein. Beasts of the mountains and of the seas of white limestone and alabaster I fashioned, and set them up in its gates, I adorned it, I made it glorious, and put copper clothes-hooks all around it. Door-leaves of cedar, cypress, juniper, and mulberry I hung in the gates thereof; and silver, gold, lead, copper, and iron, the spoil of my hand from the lands which I had brought under my sway, in great quantities I took and placed therein."

slabs following the battle scene was the triumphal return after victory. In front of the procession were warriors throwing the heads of the slain at the feet of the conquerors. Two musicians, playing on stringed instruments, preceded the charioteers, who were represented unarmed, and bearing their standards. . . . The king came next in his chariot, carrying in one hand his bow, and in the other two arrows—the attitude in which he is so frequently represented on Assyrian monuments, and probably denoting triumph over his enemies.[34]

Other noteworthy products of Assyrian artists included painted scenes, some done on brightly colored glazed bricks used to decorate the temples and palaces. Others were done on plaster, forming lively wall murals in both public buildings and private residences. Surviving examples display tremendous skill and freedom of expression and are by no means artistically inferior to the carved reliefs. Assyrian artisans also turned out beautiful metal artifacts, including bronze, silver, and gold plates, drinking vessels, and ornaments. And their work in sculpted ivory was equally fine; excavators have brought to light ivory-decorated thrones, beds, chairs, and doors, as well as ivory bowls, jewelry boxes, vases, pins, spoons, and combs, many of them inlaid with precious stones. With the notable exception of the gigantic human-headed and winged bulls and lions that guarded the palace gates and throne rooms, few free-standing statues have been found.

The Tower of Babel and Hanging Gardens

The Assyrians' archrivals, the Babylonians, also went through periods in which they produced high culture and great art. Indeed,

The skill of Assyrian bronze artisans is apparent in this figurine of a fearsome demon.

Babylonian achievements in architecture and monumental building were every bit as splendid as Assyrian ones in wall sculpture. Without doubt, at the height of the Neo-Babylonian Empire (the seventh and sixth centuries B.C.), Babylon was the greatest city in the world. A century later, the famous Greek historian Herodotus visited this metropolis on the Euphrates and wrote:

> Babylon lies in a wide plain, a vast city in the form of a square with each side nearly fourteen miles long and a circuit [outer perimeter] of some fifty-six miles, and in addition to its enormous size it surpasses in splendor any city of the known world.[35]

Of Babylon's many large-scale architectural monuments, one of the most impressive and famous was its great ziggurat, topped by a temple to the Babylonian god Marduk. Although archaeologists and historians cannot be absolutely sure, most believe that this structure gave rise to the legend of the Tower of Babel in the biblical book of Genesis. Supposedly, humans had erected the tower in an attempt to reach heaven; but God had halted the project by making them speak in different tongues, which had the effect of confusing and scattering them. If Babylon's ziggurat did inspire this tale, it was an earlier version of the building that did so. The magnificent version begun by the Neo-Babylonian king Nabopolassar and finished by his son, Nebuchadrezzar, in the sixth century B.C., was the last in a long series of restorations that stretched back for hundreds of years. It was the final and grandest restoration that Herodotus saw and described this way:

> The [courtyard of the] temple [complex] is a square building two furlongs [about 1,320 feet] each way, with bronze gates. . . . It has a solid central tower [the ziggurat itself], one furlong square, with a second erected on top of it and then a third, and so on up to eight. All eight towers can be climbed by a spiral[walk]way running round the outside, and about half-way up there are seats for those who make the ascent to rest on. On the summit of the topmost tower stands a great temple with a fine large couch in it, richly covered, and a golden table beside it.[36]

Another famous structure supposedly resting within Babylon's walls was the renowned Hanging Gardens, later called one of the seven wonders of the ancient world. In his

Library of History, the first-century B.C. Greek historian Diodorus Siculus gives this description of the monument:

> There was also, beside the acropolis [central fortress], the Hanging Garden, as it is called, which was built . . . by a later [Babylonian] king [Nebuchadrezzar] to please one of his concubines; for she, they say, being a Persian by race [she was actually Median; Diodorus here confuses Persia with Media] and longing for the meadows of her mountains, asked the king to imitate, through the artifice of a planted garden, the distinctive landscape of Persia. . . . Since the approach to the garden sloped like a hillside and the several parts of the structure rose from one another tier on tier, the appearance of the whole resembled that of a theater. When the ascending terraces had been built, there had been constructed beneath them galleries which carried the entire weight of the planted garden and rose little by little one above the other. . . . The roofs of the galleries were covered over with beams of stone sixteen foot long. . . . The roof above these beams had first a layer of reeds laid in great quantities of bitumen [tar], over this two courses of baked brick bonded by cement, and as a third layer a covering of lead, to the end that the moisture from the soil might not penetrate beneath. On all this again the earth had been piled to the depth sufficient for the roots of the largest trees; and the ground . . . was thickly planted with trees of every

kind. . . . And since the galleries . . . all received the light, they contained many royal lodges of every description; and there was one gallery which contained openings leading from . . . machines for supplying the gardens with water, the machines raising the water in great abundance from the river.[37]

Archaeologists have long searched for the remains of this fabled structure. One idea, that the great ziggurat described by Herodotus was once covered by greenery and was therefore the Hanging Gardens,

has been discounted. German archaeologist Robert Koldewey, the principal initial excavator of Babylon, suggested that a structure known as the Vaulted Building was the Hanging Gardens. But later scholars have concluded that the Vaulted Building was more likely a storehouse for cuneiform tablets. A more recent guess, by University of London Assyriologist D. J. Wiseman, places the famed gardens on terraces erected on a massive outer wall near the Euphrates River. For the moment, the exact location of this monument remains uncertain.

This modern reconstruction of Babylon, with the Hanging Gardens in the foreground and the Tower of Babel in the distance, is fanciful; but the level of splendor depicted is probably accurate.

Babylon's Mighty Walls

Far more certain, productive, and informative were Koldewey's excavations of Babylon's famous outer defensive walls and their system of fortified towers. The city's original walls had been rebuilt many times over the centuries; those that Koldewey unearthed, the most impressive of all, were the work of Nebuchadrezzar. In his 1914 work, *The Excavations at Babylon*, Koldewey described two walls, each about twenty-three feet thick, running parallel to each other and separated by an open space of about forty feet. At the top of the outer wall, he found a roadway wide enough for two four-horse chariots to

traverse at the same time, a stunning confirmation of the descriptions of Herodotus and other ancient writers. (Koldewey concluded that this roadway made it possible to move large numbers of troops quite speedily to a section of the defenses that was under attack.)

Koldewey's excavations, which began in 1899 and lasted almost eighteen years, revealed that numerous fortified guard towers existed at intervals along these walls. "Up to the present," he wrote in 1914,

> we have found about 15 of the towers. . . . They . . . project [outward] both at the front and the back, thus

This photo shows the remains of some of the surviving sections of Babylon's massive outer perimeter of defensive walls, excavated by Germany's Robert Koldewey.

HERODOTUS ON BABYLON'S WALLS

In this excerpt from his famous history (Aubrey de Sélincourt's translation), the ancient Greek historian Herodotus describes the massive walls of Babylon, which he saw with his own eyes when he traveled through the Near East in the late 450s B.C. Modern archaeologists have confirmed most of his details.

"It [the city] is surrounded by a broad deep moat full of water, and within the moat there is a wall fifty cubits wide and two hundred high [a cubit being the approximate distance from the elbow to the fingertips, or about twenty inches]. . . . While the digging [of the moat] was going on, the earth that was shoveled out was formed into bricks, which were baked in ovens as soon as a sufficient number were made; then, using hot bitumen [petroleum] for mortar, the workmen began by supporting the moat's sides with brick, and then went on to erect the actual wall. . . . On the top of the wall they constructed, along each edge, a row of one-roomed buildings facing inwards with enough space between for a four-horse chariot to pass. There are a hundred gates in the circuit of the wall, all of bronze with bronze uprights [vertical supports] and lintels [horizontal top pieces]."

placed astride on the wall. They were, of course, higher than the walls, but we can get no clue from the ruins as to the height of the walls or towers, as only the lower parts remain. The towers are 3.36 meters [about 11 feet] wide and are placed 44 meters [about 144 feet] apart. Thus, on the entire front there were about 90, and on the whole circumference—provided the town formed a square—there must have been 360 towers.[38]

These mighty walls could not have been raised without an ambitious, committed, and energetic national leader, talented architects, and an industrious workforce. Their remains, along with those of Babylon's great ziggurat and other architectural wonders, attest to the uncommon achievements of a remarkable people in an equally remarkable age.

CHAPTER FOUR

OF PEASANTS AND KINGS: MESOPOTAMIAN SOCIAL ORGANIZATION

Since the days of Botta, Layard, and other early pioneers, archaeologists have tried to piece together a credible, detailed picture of the society (government, priesthood, social classes, slaves, and so forth) of a typical Mesopotamian empire. The term typical can be fairly safely applied here mainly because the various cultures of ancient Mesopotamia were largely homogeneous (of a similar nature) from a political and social standpoint. A useful analogy would be Europe in the Middle Ages and early modern times. Although different ruling houses from different parts of Europe dominated parts or most of the continent from one century to another, they were all more or less culturally the same in that they were white, Christian, had the same kind of government (monarchy), the same social structure (made up of nobles, soldiers, merchants, and peasants), the same agricultural methods, marriage customs, and so forth.

So it was in Mesopotamia, in which the various kingdoms and empires based their political and social structures mainly on old Sumerian models. Cultural ideas and customs thus traditionally flowed northwest-

ward from the original Sumerian heartland, near the Persian Gulf, into central and northern Mesopotamia, the area in which the Assyrian Empire was eventually centered. In the early second millennium B.C., following the decline of the Sumerians, Babylon became the heir to and repository of Sumerian culture; and thereafter it set Mesopotamia's cultural and social standards. Interestingly, though the more warlike Assyria was often Babylonia's rival and conqueror, certain influential Assyrian factions felt perfectly comfortable continuing this trend. As A. Leo Oppenheim points out, "There were circles in Assyria which looked toward Babylonia for an example and for the formation of a self-image."[39] Balancing this attitude was a strong anti-Babylonian faction in Assyria that kept alive native traditions and feelings of patriotism and nationalism. (This love-hate relationship between Assyria and Babylonia was comparable to the later one between Rome and Greece; in each case, a nation of warriors borrowed many of its social and cultural ideas from the weaker but more refined neighbor it had conquered.)

Historians have used a variety of sources to illuminate the classes and other organization of ancient Sumerian, Babylonian, and Assyrian society. Of paramount importance are the royal annals and other official descriptions of military campaigns and construction projects, the traditional mode of expression of the kings. Besides these accounts, a number of personal letters, legal contracts, and religious and scientific compositions have survived on tablets found in royal archives. The largest such collection was discovered in 1849 by Layard at Nineveh. Consisting of more than twenty-five thousand cuneiform tablets, it constituted the bulk of the library gathered by the Assyrian monarch Assurbanipal.

Though valuable, most of these records deal with political, religious, and commercial affairs in royal, official, priestly, and well-to-do circles, and tell very little about the everyday lives of average people. As Georges Roux remarks, "Numerous and interesting as these texts are . . . the knowledge that can be derived from them on such topics as social and economic conditions, land tenure and internal trade, for example, remains very limited and full of gaps and uncertainties."[40]

Most of the impressive public buildings in ancient Babylon, as captured in this modern drawing, were used by the royal and priestly classes. Most of the people were peasants who lived in humble abodes.

53

A "MONSTER" RISES FROM THE EARTH

The nature of royal courts, social classes, and other aspects of ancient Mesopotamian society would have remained a mystery had it not been for the diligent work of generations of archaeologists. As this excerpt from Layard's classic *Nineveh and Its Remains* shows, among the many difficulties early excavators encountered was convincing local workers that there was nothing to fear from some of the more imposing artifacts that were unearthed.

"I was returning to the mound [containing the ruins of an Assyrian palace], when I saw two Arabs . . . coming towards me and urging on their mares to the top of their speed. "Hasten!" . . . exclaimed one of them—"hasten to the diggers, for they have found Nimrud himself! . . . There is no God but God!"; and both joining in this pious exclamation, they galloped off. . . . On reaching the ruins, I descended into the newly opened trench, and found the workmen. . . . [They showed me] an enormous human head sculptured in full out of the alabaster [a finely grained white stone] of the country. They had uncovered the upper part of a figure, the remainder of which was still buried in the earth. I at once saw that the head must belong to a winged lion or bull. . . . I was not surprised that the Arabs had been amazed and terrified at this apparition. It required no stretch of imagination to conjure up the most strange fancies. This gigantic head . . . rising from the bowels of the earth, might well have belonged to one of those fearful beings which are described in the traditions of the country as appearing to mortals, slowly ascending from the regions below. One of the workmen, on catching the first glimpse of the monster, had thrown down his basket and run [away] as fast as his legs could carry him."

To fill in these gaps, historians consult the works of Hebrew, Greek, Roman, and other non-Mesopotamian ancient writers who described Mesopotamia, its peoples, and its society (for example, Herodotus's description of Babylon); and archaeologists study the ruins of houses, temples, and others buildings, as well as surviving tools, fragments of pottery, statues, steles bearing inscriptions, and other material artifacts.

The Monarch and His Heir

The most logical place to begin in attempting to reconstruct ancient Mesopotamian society is the social sphere that scholars know the most about—namely, the king's court and imperial administration. In this regard, a great deal is known about the Assyrian kings and their court (thanks to the royal archives and extensive wall sculptures discovered in the ruins of Assyria's royal palaces). It is a fair assumption that the social status and government of these kings strongly resembled those of other Mesopotamian rulers, ranging from Akkad's Sargon (late third millennium B.C.) to Babylonia's Nebuchadrezzar (mid–first millennium B.C.).

The Assyrian monarch was seen as a human being rather than as a god in human form (as were most Egyptian pharaohs). Yet as the earthly representative and instrument of the gods, he was no ordinary human. Official texts frequently mention an aura or radiance surrounding his person, the *melammu*, or "awe-inspiring luminosity." This was presumably a supernatural force that supposedly flowed directly from the god. Because of this special relationship with the divine, the king was the chief god's highest priest as well as the supreme head of state. For the sake of the community, it was believed, such a special person had to be closely guarded and pampered. "His person was carefully protected from disease," Oppenheim explains,

Ur-Nammu (left), king of Ur, approaches the god Sin to request permission to build a temple. Mesopotamian monarchs were seen as having special relationships with the gods.

and especially from the evil influence of magic because his well-being was considered essential for that of the country. For this reason, Assyrian kings, as we know from the letters in their archives, were surrounded by a host of diviners [those claiming to be able to foretell the future by interpreting various signs] and physicians. All ominous signs were observed and interpreted with regard to their bearing on the royal person. Complex rituals existed to ward off evil signs, and at least one instance is known in Assyria where a fatal prediction was counteracted by the stratagem of making another person king . . . for one hundred days and then killing and duly burying him so that the omen should be fulfilled but fate cheated and the true king kept alive. Access to the king was carefully regulated, even for the heir apparent, to avoid untoward [adverse] encounters, and in each Assyrian palace was a room, adjacent to the throne room, for ritual ablutions [cleansings] of the king.[41]

The "heir apparent" was most often the king's son, the crown prince. Although the king's choice of a son as his successor was supposedly inspired by the gods, that choice had to be endorsed by other members of the royal family as well as by the nation's small elite group of noblemen. Most often these highborn people went along with the king's selection. (One notable exception was a power struggle that erupted among the sons of the Assyrian king Sennacherib after he was murdered.)

Once chosen and accepted, the Assyrian crown prince left his father's palace and

King Assurbanipal hunts a lion in this detail from a relief found in his palace.

resided in the "House of Succession," located a few miles upstream from Nineveh. There the young man learned arts and letters, received instruction in kingly duties, and prepared to replace his father at a moment's notice in case the reigning monarch should die in battle. Assurbanipal's annals contain this description of his own youthful training:

The art of the Master Adapa I learned—the hidden treasure of all scribal knowledge, the signs of heaven and earth. I was brave, I was exceedingly industrious . . . and I have studied the heavens with the learned masters of oil divination, I have solved the laborious problems of division and multiplication . . . I have read the artistic script of Sumer and the obscure Akkadian, which is hard to master. . . . I mounted my steed, I rode joyfully . . . I held the bow, I shot the arrow, the sign of my valor. I hurled heavy lances like a javelin.

Holding the reins like a driver, I made the [chariot's] wheels go round. . . . At the same time I was learning royal decorum, walking in the kingly ways . . . giving commands to the nobles. . . . The father, my begetter, saw for himself the bravery which the great gods decreed as my portion.[42]

Warrior, Lawgiver, and Priest

Each royal prince eventually faced his day of reckoning, the moment when his father "went to his destiny." The fallen king was placed in a heavy stone sarcophagus and entombed. Then, following a short interval, the prince's

coronation ceremony took place and his nobles and officials paid him homage, after which there was probably a good deal of public rejoicing. Having assumed the throne, the new king found that his life was, in a sense, no longer his own, for his duties were many and diverse. First and foremost, of course, he was the supreme commander of the army, with the authority to initiate wars at his will and to draw up plans for his military campaigns. By tradition, he also made sure army rations were distributed properly, inspected the troops, and often personally led campaigns.

At court, the king appointed governors and other administrators, received and entertained

Assyrian and other Mesopotamian kings were the supreme military commanders and sometimes even fought in battles. Depicted here are some of King Assurbanipal's Elamite enemies.

high officials and foreign ambassadors, and dealt with a wide range of appeals and complaints by his subjects. These appeals dealt with their rights in such matters as land ownership, access to water for irrigation, protection against economic exploitation by other citizens, and of course protection against brigands and foreign invaders. "It was a primary function of the ruler to defend these rights," H. W. F. Saggs explains. "So long as he did so, he received the support of the citizenry."[43]

It was also the king's duty to uphold the law and mete out justice. The ruler was expected "to see to it that the poor and the weak were not oppressed," Samuel Kramer writes,

> that widows and orphans were not victimized, [and] that the ordinary citizen did not suffer at the hands of overbearing and corrupt officials. To make people aware of their legal rights and thus help to prevent the miscarriage of justice, kings promulgated [officially announced] regulations, edicts, and law codes.[44]

The most famous of Mesopotamia's law codes was that created by the great eighteenth-century B.C. Babylonian king Hammurabi, which contained nearly three hundred laws. It was discovered in 1902 by a team of French archaeologists who were digging in the ruins of Susa. (Originally the capital of the Elamite kingdom, Susa and its environs were later incorporated into various Babylonian, Assyrian, and other Near Eastern empires. The stone bearing the law code was transported to the city about the year 1200 B.C. by an Elamite king after he had looted the Babylonian town of Sippar.) Once they realized what they had found, the excited excavators handed the

roughly thirty-five hundred lines of text over to a translator. Since that time, fragments of other copies of Hammurabi's law code have been discovered by diggers at other Mesopotamian sites.

In addition to having to handle so many military, courtly, and administrative duties, as well as dispense justice, a king like Hammurabi was also expected to execute his duties as the empire's supreme high priest. These included seeing that temples were built or maintained, appointing the regular priests, leading various religious ceremonies and festivals, and conducting numerous complicated rituals connected with omens, divination, astrology, and magic. A beautiful bas-relief erected by Assurbanipal (and excavated by Layard at Nineveh) shows that great Assyrian king in his role as high priest, pouring wine (a liquid sacrifice called a libation) over the heads of some dead lions. Meanwhile, his attendants play sacred music on a harp and incense burns atop a nearby pillar. An inscription, carved in cuneiform above the scene, reads:

> Upon the lions which I slew, I rested the fierce bow of the goddess Ishtar. I offered a sacrifice over them and poured on them a libation of wine. The great gods, in their council, caused me to attain unto the priesthood, which I desired. The offerings I brought were pleasing unto them. The sanctuaries of the great gods, my lords, I restored.[45]

Nobles and Priests

Although all power in a Mesopotamian empire theoretically resided in the king, to run that realm he naturally had to delegate some of his authority to the rich nobles who made up the tiny but highly influential upper class. These included members of the priesthood, high military officers, important dignitaries (such as the palace herald), royal advisers and administrators, provincial governors, district chiefs, and town "mayors." All of these highly

MESOPOTAMIA'S MOST FAMOUS LAW CODE

Hammurabi's law code, which was based to some degree on earlier Sumerian and Akkadian regulations, influenced the justice systems of many later Mesopotamian peoples. Here (from a translation in Bailkey's *Readings in Ancient History*) are a few of the code's 282 known laws.

"1. If a man brings an accusation against another man, charging him with murder, but cannot prove it, the accuser shall be put to death. . . .

5. If a judge pronounce a judgment, render a decision, [or] deliver a verdict duly signed and sealed, and afterward alter his judgment, they shall call that judge to account . . . and he shall pay twelve-fold the penalty in that judgment. . . .

22. If a man practices robbery and is captured, that man shall be put to death.

23. If the robber is not captured, the man who has been robbed shall, in the presence of god, make an itemized statement of his loss, and the city and the governor in whose province . . . the robbery was committed shall compensate him for whatever he has lost. . . .

55. If a man opens his canal for irrigation and neglects it and the water carries away an adjacent field, he shall pay out grain on the basis of the adjacent field. . . .

109. If bad characters gather in the house of a wine seller and she does not arrest those bad characters and bring them to the palace, that wine seller shall be put to death. . . .

195. If a son strikes his father, they shall cut off his hand.

196. If a man destroys the eye of another man, they shall destroy his eye. . . .

229. If a builder builds a house for a man and does not make its construction sound, and the house he has built collapses and causes the death of the owner . . . that builder shall be put to death."

ership, consisting of royal estates, temple estates, and family estates.

As might be expected, the temple estates were controlled and run by members of the priesthood, who made up a small but prominent element of privileged society. By the late third millennium B.C., many of the temples scattered across Mesopotamia had grown into large compounds—diverse collections of shrines, storehouses, residences, meeting halls, and other buildings. The wealth accumulated by such estates and controlled by their priests was the product of a special social-religious relationship they enjoyed with the monarch, who was, of course, looked on as the highest priest in the land. "The building and constant maintenance of the sanctuaries [temple compounds] was a royal . . . obligation," comments Oppenheim.

> From victorious kings the temple expected a share in the [war] booty, especially precious votive gifts to be exhibited to the deity in the cella [the temple's most sacred inner chamber] and the dedication of prisoners of war to increase the labor force of the temple. Under the tutelage of the priests, from the Old Babylonian period [the time of Hammurabi] onward, kings were made to see that the building of larger and more sumptuously [magnificently] decorated sanctuaries with higher temple towers was an essential part of their duty toward the god, an expression of thanks, as well as a guarantee of future successes.[46]

A surviving fresco depicts two Assyrian nobles, perhaps high royal administrators.

placed individuals led privileged lives, of course, residing in comfortable houses staffed by many servants and owning their own lands.

The way the members of the privileged class obtained their lands reveals a good deal about the structure of Mesopotamian society. In theory, all land in Assyria, Babylonia, and other Mesopotamian states belonged to the king or the religious temples. In practice, however, the ruler and/or the temples granted high-placed persons estates as part of a reward system designed to maintain their continued homage and obedience. Although legally speaking such lands still belonged to the king or temples, most of the time they became hereditary holdings, passed from father to son. Thus, there developed what historians refer to as the tripartite (three-part) system of land own-

This privileged class of priests was divided into its own hierarchy (ladder of status and authority). The high priests (and in some cases priestesses) had the most authority, followed by those priests with specialized skills and duties; some were trained to conduct one of several specific kinds of ceremonies, for example, while others were adept at interpreting omens, supernatural signs of impending good or bad fortune. Below the priests themselves were various temple administrators, maintenance people, and ser- vants, all of whom were essential in the upkeep of these complex and socially important temple estates.

As a rule, these and other estates in the tripartite system were not huge contiguous tracts worked by thousands of slaves, like those that developed in Roman Italy several centuries later. Most Mesopotamian estates

A modern reconstruction shows peasant workers erecting a temple. In the system of forced labor that was common in the ancient Near East, such public work was a form of taxation.

A CITIZEN PLEADS FOR JUSTICE

A good many of the appeals that Mesopotamian subjects made to their kings were no doubt pleas for them to dispense justice. This excerpt from a surviving letter (printed in Oppenheim's *Letters from Mesopotamia*), made to one of Assyria's greatest kings, Assurbanipal, is an example of such a plea.

"How does it happen that I, who have made several appeals to Your Majesty, have never been questioned by anybody? It is as if . . . I had committed a crime against Your Majesty. But I have not committed a crime against Your Majesty; I merely went . . . and conveyed an order of the king to Arrabi; although I said, 'I am on business for the palace,' he was so unscrupulous as to take my property away. He even arrested me and put me in fetters [shackles, or restraints], and that in front of all the people. . . . Ever since last year, nobody has given me anything to eat. . . . Your Majesty should know that the same two men who took the gold jewelry from around my neck still go on planning to destroy me and to ruin me, and what terrible words about me have they made reach the ears of Your Majesty!"

were relatively moderate in size, the largest covering only about 250 acres, although a well-to-do landlord might own several such properties scattered across the empire in which he resided. Typically, except for the priests on the temple estates, landlords were absentee, meaning that they lived in a town or city and entrusted the upkeep of the property to a paid manager.

The Laboring Classes

Evidently the labor utilized by estate owners and managers consisted of a mixture of free agricultural workers, serfs, and perhaps a few slaves. Unfortunately the differences among these groups, as well as their precise social status and distribution, remain somewhat unclear. Some free workers seem to have be-

come potters, metalworkers, and other kinds of craftspeople in the cities; others appear to have hired themselves out as laborers on the large estates run by the kings, temples, or nobles. Some free workers probably also owned their own small plots of land; but they paid high taxes, which the government usually exacted in the form of "forced labor" rather than money. Forced labor, a common practice across the Near East, "was seen by administrators," Daniel Snell points out, "as a way of taxing peasants without having to resort to forms of money, and sometimes it was used to concentrate labor resources on a magnificent scale and to accomplish in a few years projects that otherwise might have taken generations."[47] Thus, after planting season, many free Mesopotamian peasants must have worked off their tax burdens by devoting a few months to erecting palaces, digging canals, and other state projects.

On the other hand, slaves and serfs had little or no say at all in the work they did. There were three ways a person became a slave in ancient Mesopotamia. He or she might be a foreigner captured in a raid or war, a foreigner bought by a slave trader and sold to a local citizen, or a free citizen who was reduced to the status of slave after falling heavily into debt. A slave's lowly status was not necessarily permanent, however, for most slaves evidently received small wages for their labor and could attempt to buy their freedom; or a slave might be granted freedom by his or her owner out of kindness or for some other reason. In any case, compared with the later large-scale slavery institutions of ancient Rome and the pre–Civil War United States, slavery in ancient Mesopotamian societies was mostly small-scale and had little economic importance. "Police power was minimal," Snell explains,

> and these societies were not prepared to adopt the constant vigilance necessary for a slave society to flourish. . . . Most rich households probably had from one to five personal slaves . . . but rarely did the number of slaves owned go above fifteen. Because of their propensity to run away, slaves could not efficiently be used for agricultural work, and few attempts were made in that direction.[48]

Ancient Mesopotamian societies also featured people of low social status who fell somewhere between a free laborer and a slave. The term "serf" is often used to describe these workers. However, as Snell points out:

This carved relief from Nineveh depicts the residents of a captured town being led away into slavery. This was perhaps the most common way that people became slaves.

The term "serf" is probably too imprecise . . . because it conjures up a European feudal system in which the peasants were not only attached to the land and had duties and taxes to render to a lord, but also could count on the lord's political and military protection. In spite of various efforts to find feudalism in the ancient Near East, no one has demonstrated any-

Most of the people of ancient Mesopotamia were poor peasants; however, a few, including a small middle class of merchants, like those seen here, were able to make comfortable livings.

thing like the European [version of this institution] in any ancient Near Eastern society. What has been documented is that in many periods soldiers and other government officials were paid at least in part by being given allotments of land by the government. . . . The officials did not then have judicial authority over the peasants who worked the land. From the point of view of the government, such a practice was extremely attractive. Taxes did not have to be collected, and yet the soldiers were fed.[49]

Whatever the differences among these various kinds of lower-class laborers, it is certain that they had at least one thing in common. Like poor peasants in every age, they were all regularly exploited in one way or another by the upper classes.

Taking Advantage of Social Mobility

So far, the social classes considered have been either highly privileged or of modest means and/or low status. As in many lands in many ages, there were also people in ancient Mesopotamia who might be termed middle class. But one must be careful not to equate this group with the numerically large and politically and economically influential middle classes that exist in modern developed nations like the United States, England, and France. The fact is that the vast majority of the inhabitants of Babylonia, Assyria, and other Mesopotamian empires were poor and had no political power, while a very tiny percentage of privileged persons held almost all the political and economic clout. According to Saggs, "Power was concentrated within three groups: the king, the temple authorities, and senior members of ancient or wealthy families [i.e., the nobles]."[50]

Still, there existed a fair amount of social mobility in these empires, which meant that under some circumstances a person could change his or her social status and economic situation. "A man who began landless could become a landowner," Saggs points out, "[and] the slave could be granted his freedom."[51] Similarly, a royal administrator who worked hard and pleased the king might be rewarded with a generous grant of land, significantly increasing his status and wealth; or a trader or merchant who was uncommonly diligent or lucky in business might become well-off and be able to afford to buy his own plots of land. Such a person was not highborn and therefore did not have noble status, yet neither was he a peasant, so he fell somewhere between the two extremes.

A few unusually successful farmers, artisans, and scribes also fell into this middle class, whose members could afford to own comfortable homes and perhaps a few slaves. But though individually prosperous, these people were relatively few in number and had no significant political impact in the age of the great Mesopotamian empires. A well-known exception was the legendary Sargon of Akkad. He was said to have taken the fullest possible advantage of prevailing social mobility by rising to the kingship from humble origins. Here, then, was that rare member of Mesopotamian society who knew what it was like to be both a peasant and a king.

CHAPTER FIVE

ASPECTS OF EVERYDAY LIFE IN ANCIENT MESOPOTAMIA

The manner in which a person lived in ancient Mesopotamia depended on two crucial factors. The first factor was *where* he or she lived. As has been the case throughout most of recorded history, some people dwelled in the countryside, and others inhabited towns or cities. And not surprisingly, the differences were marked between rural life in open, sparsely inhabited plains and marshes and urban life in cities with narrow streets lined by densely packed dwellings. The kind and quality of one's life also depended on social status and wealth. The vast majority of people, both rural and urban dwellers, worked long days, year after year, to acquire what today would be regarded as basic minimum sustenance and comforts; whereas the relatively few members of the upper classes, like their counterparts in all ages and places, enjoyed far more comfortable and secure lives.

Unfortunately, much more is known about the lives of Mesopotamia's handful of well-to-do individuals than about those of the far more numerous members of the lower classes. Archaeologists and other scholars long ago learned that most of the surviving evidence for ancient societies and how people in them lived relates to the upper classes. This is partly because ancient writers, scribes, record keepers, sculptors, and so forth were usually either members of the privileged classes or worked for them. So what they wrote or carved into stone dealt primarily with the lives of the rich, famous, and powerful; and their references to members of the lower classes tended to be few and superficial. The old Sumerian proverb "The poor men are the silent men in Sumer"[52] may have originally referred to the underprivileged having no political clout. But it could just as well be applied to the silence about them and their lives in the ancient records.

Archaeologists try to make up for this disparity in the surviving written records by excavating the homes, tools, graves, and other artifacts of the less privileged members of Mesopotamian society. But here again, the advantages of the wealthy are telling. Only they could afford to erect mighty brick and stone fortresses, palaces, temples, and so on, buildings that by their very size have managed, to some degree, to withstand the ravages of time. The humble mud, reed, and thatch dwellings of the poor, by contrast, have for the most part deteriorated and disappeared.

Hunters of the Marshlands

Luckily though, archaeologists and other scholars attempting to reconstruct the lives of the poorer ancient Mesopotamians have been aided by the fact that the dwellings, tools, and daily routines of some people in the Near East have changed little over the millennia. In a broad band of marshlands located near the confluence of the Tigris and Euphrates Rivers, for example, small tribal groups still eke out the same minimal livings their distant ancestors did. And by closely observing these modern marsh dwellers, scholars have learned a great deal about their ancient counterparts. "Their lives follow patterns established sixty centuries ago," Samuel Kramer writes,

> in the days when the first nomadic tribes settled in this watery land. Like their distant predecessors, the men of the marshes catch fish in the lagoons, bake unleavened bread in crude ovens, herd water buffalo, and build arched huts of towering reeds. . . . The round of their daily lives is an echo of an age when arts were rudimentary, history unwritten, and cities not yet known.[53]

These people of the marshlands build their huts from reeds out of necessity. This is because Mesopotamia's marshy areas, just as

in ages past, are devoid of large trees or quarries to supply wood or stone. The chief method of constructing such a hut is to tie clusters of tall reeds into thick, sturdy bundles and then dig holes and sink the ends of the bundles into the ground. The bundles, which now stand upright like columns, are bent over and their tops attached to the tops of other bundles, forming arches. Crosspieces, also made of bundled reeds, connect and brace the arches, after which thick reed mats are tied to the top and sides, forming the hut's roof and walls.

The light narrow boats these marsh dwellers use to catch fish and water fowl,

The lifestyle of these modern Arab marsh dwellers is similar to that of their ancient ancestors.

their main food supply, are also constructed of reeds. Most of the modern hunters in the region have come to use guns to kill their prey. But as late as the mid–twentieth century, many of them still employed the age-old methods, in which the hunters stood upright in their boats, wielding long bamboo poles with metal tips. They then speared ducks, heron, and other birds, as well as eels and various kinds of fish.

Farmers and Their Crops

Most of the other rural poor in ancient Mesopotamia, constituting a large proportion of the total population, were farmers and herders who lived in the plains and low foothills. Their dwellings, often as humble as those of the people of the marshlands, were frequently organized into small villages. The most primitive houses were circular huts made of intertwined branches covered with thatch and loosely cemented with dried mud. The wooden or thatched door hung on a pivot secured to a post driven into the ground or attached to the wall. Stables and sheepfolds were also constructed using this method. Somewhat more permanent homes

were fashioned from bricks made of clay that had been mixed with straw and either dried in the sun or baked in a kiln. Baked bricks were sturdier and lasted longer, but they were more expensive to produce and so their use was generally restricted to the larger homes of the well-to-do or to state building projects.[54]

Since prehistoric times, small farmers had managed to feed themselves and sustain their villages in Mesopotamia. Then, beginning in the late fourth and early third millennia B.C. when the first large cities began to rise, many of these rural folk migrated into the growing urban centers. Their burgeoning populations required a great deal of food, which of course had to be imported from the countryside; and that greatly increased the importance of and demands on the remaining farmers in the areas surrounding the cities.

The crop most widely cultivated by these farmers was barley, a type of wheat that grows well in Mesopotamia's somewhat salty soil. People either used the barley kernels to make a thick porridge or ground them into flour to make a flat bread that is still popular

A vignette from ancient Mesopotamian farm life is captured in this temple relief showing workers milking cows. Farmers and herders made up the bulk of the population.

in most parts of the Near East. They also made a nutritious and tasty beer from the barley. Other common food crops included lentils, peas, beans, garlic, cucumbers, lettuce, apples, figs, and grapes.

Mesopotamian farmers became very adept at following methods and a yearly timetable for planting and harvesting that produced the most plentiful crop yields. One of the most important and revealing discoveries made by twentieth-century archaeologists in the Near East is what has come to be known as the "Farmer's Almanac." A set of instructions designed to guide farmers in proper planting and harvesting, it was pieced together from more than a dozen fragments, one of which Leonard Wooley unearthed while excavating at Ur. Samuel Kramer subsequently made a translation, a particularly difficult job considering that the text contained several technical terms no one had seen before. In the excerpt that follows, note that the anonymous author describes a sophisticated form of irrigation channels and dikes that were common across much of ancient Mesopotamia.

> When you are about to take hold of your field (for cultivation), keep a sharp eye on the opening of the dikes, ditches, and mounds (so that) when you flood the field the water will not rise too high in it. When you have emptied it of water, watch the field's water-soaked ground that it stay virile [fertile] ground for you. Let shod oxen (that is, oxen whose hooves are protected in one way or another) trample it for you; (and) after having its weeds ripped out (by them) (and) the field made level ground, dress it evenly with narrow axes weighing (no more

The bottom panel in this detail from the Standard of Ur shows herders driving cattle and sheep.

> than) two-thirds of a pound each. [Then] let the pickax wielder eradicate [the marks left by] the ox hooves for you (and) smooth them out. . . . When you are about to plow your field, keep your eye on the man who puts in the barley seed. Let him drop the grain uniformly two fingers deep (and) use up one shekel of barley for each *garush*.[55]

The oxen used for plowing were among the domesticated animals bred on farms. Much less expensive to breed and maintain and far more numerous in the region were sheep and goats. Sheep, which were essential to the production of wool for clothes and also an important food source, were perhaps most numerous of all. Small flocks tended by shepherds, often adolescents and even younger children doing their part for the family's welfare, could be seen everywhere in the countryside; and the large wealthy estates kept flocks numbering in the thousands.

City Dwellings

Not surprisingly, most of the tremendous output of food, wool, and other commodities produced in the countryside was destined for the cities. Compared to the mainly rural societies of Greece, Italy, and most other populated areas in the second and early first millennium B.C., Mesopotamia was highly urbanized; that is, it had many towns with populations in the tens of thousands. Both before and after the rise of the great empires, people tended to have great pride in their native cities, as exemplified in these lines from Gilgamesh's epic, boasting of the impressive walls of the renowned Uruk:

This pottery model gives a clear idea of the form of the typical modest Mesopotamian house.

> Look at it still today. The outer wall where the cornice runs, it shines with the brilliance of copper; and the inner wall, it has no equal. . . . Climb upon the wall of Uruk; walk along it, I say; regard the foundation terrace and examine the building; is it not burnt brick and good?[56]

Inside the circuits of their defensive walls, the centers of these cities were dominated by imposing temples, often atop high ziggurats, and sometimes the magnificent palaces of the kings. Around such large-scale structures stretched wide clusters of closely packed mud-brick houses, shops, stables, and storerooms, separated at intervals by narrow winding streets. The average house was fairly unimpressive; it most often consisted of a modest open-air courtyard with a few small windowless rooms surrounding it, all enclosed by a wall for privacy and security.

By contrast, some townhouses, including those of absentee landlords, government administrators, well-to-do merchants, and other better-off citizens, were much larger and more comfortable. Kramer describes such a house as

> a two-story structure made of the kiln-baked and sun-dried brick, neatly whitewashed inside and out. . . . From a small entrance vestibule [hallway] one stepped down into a brick-paved court provided with a central drain to carry off water during the winter rainy season. Opening off the court were the doors to the ground-floor rooms. The number of these rooms might vary from house to house, but typically they consisted of a chamber where guests were received and entertained . . . a lavatory [bathroom]; the kitchen with its fireplaces . . . a servants' room; and a general workroom. . . . A flight of stairs led up to the second story, where a wooden gallery about three feet wide . . . ran around the courtyard, leading to the family's private living quarters. A ladder probably gave access to the flat . . . roof, on which the family often slept on clear summer nights.[57]

The furnishings of such homes would be fairly familiar to most people today. There were beds, couches, tables and chairs, wooden chests for storing clothes, rugs on the floors, and brightly colored decorations on the walls.

Sanitation, Disease, and Medicine

But if their personal furnishings were almost modern in style, the sanitary practices of Mesopotamian city dwellers were decidedly primitive by modern standards. Water, for both washing and drinking, usually came from rivers (which explains why the majority of cities were erected alongside or very near rivers); needless to say, unfiltered river water can carry a number of parasites and diseases. (One exception to the rule was Assyria, where by the first millennium B.C. a good many towns had their own wells, which supplied much cleaner, safer water.) Also, the townhouses of ordinary workers and peasants had no bathrooms; neither were there any communal toilets. So large numbers of people commonly relieved themselves in the small orchards and gardens that existed within a city's walls.

In addition, people routinely threw their garbage and other refuse into the streets. There, pigs, dogs, and rats roamed in considerable numbers, eating their fill. But though they may have eliminated a fair amount of the garbage, these scavengers could not remove the danger of disease—including tiny worms that humans acquired by ingesting undercooked pork (the same pigs that ate the garbage!) and bubonic plague, spread by fleas that infested the rats. "Conditions were ideal for the outbreak of epidemics," Saggs writes.

Epidemic disease was such an accepted part of the scheme of things that there were prominent plague gods, whose duty was to punish cities by this affliction. The [Akkadian] word for epidemic disease was *mutanu*, meaning literally something like "certain death.". . . Akkadian texts abound with references to *mutanu*. . . . An omen speaks of plague gods marching with the troops, perhaps a reference to typhus. . . . Other texts speak of affected cities with daily deaths, whole countries hit by fatal epidemics, and epidemics continuing for years.[58]

Mesopotamian doctors were almost certainly unable to combat such epidemics, mostly because they had no concept of germs and the ways in which they spread infection. Sumerian, Assyrian, and Babylonian physicians believed that sickness and disease were inflicted by the gods to punish human sins;

Disease was thought to be a punishment sent by a god, such as the one shown here seated on a throne.

or that the gods might allow demons to take control of a person's body; or that sorcerers and witches could cast spells on people. Not surprisingly, magical rites, incantations, prayers, and sacrifices were the principal remedies in this traditional magical-religious brand of medicine, referred to as *ashiputu*.

At least by the eighth century B.C., however, a few doctors also practiced a more practical kind of medicine, called *asutu*. Although they too believed in divine wrath and evil demons, and certainly knew nothing about the existence of germs, they did recognize that some sickness is caused by natural agents such as dust, spoiled food or drink, or infectious "contagion." And they accordingly attempted to treat some patients with various drugs, herbs, ointments, and perhaps some simple kinds of surgery. This fresh approach used by such practical healers represents the first stirrings of true scientific inquiry based on evidence and cause and effect, which would begin to find fuller expression a few centuries later in Greece.

A WIDESPREAD ARRAY OF SUPERSTITIONS

The idea that disease was caused by the gods, demons, or evil spells was only part of a traditional belief system that included omens, curses, exorcisms, astrology, and other forms of superstition and magic. These are excerpts from letters (quoted in Oppenheim's *Letters from Mesopotamia*) that were written by some seventh-century B.C. Assyrian priests to their king, Esarhaddon. They show clearly that such superstition existed at society's highest levels.

"As to Your Majesty's request addressed to me concerning the incident with the ravens, here are the relevant omens: 'If a raven brings something into a person's house, this man will obtain something that does not belong to him. If a falcon or a raven drops something he is carrying upon a person's house or in front of a man, this house will have much traffic—traffic means profit. If a bird carries meat, another bird, or anything else, and drops it upon a person's house, this man will obtain a large inheritance.'

As to Your Majesty's writing to me concerning the ritual, they should perform the exorcistic ritual [to chase away a demon] exactly as Your Majesty did several times already. As to . . . the formulas [spells] to be pronounced, the king should watch the formulas carefully. The king should not eat what has been cooked on fire; he should put on a loose robe of a nurse; the day after tomorrow he should go down to the river to wash himself. The king should perform the ritual . . . several times."

Workers and Women

Doctors, like priests, scribes, and other persons seen as highly skilled, were few in number. Far more numerous were the ordinary workers who made up the majority of city populations. A few of these residents probably worked those plots of farmland that lay directly outside the city walls. But most other urban dwellers labored inside the city walls, as artisans, traders, shopkeepers, and "factory" workers. The factories were apparently state-run workrooms in which small or large groups of people wove carpets, embroidered clothes, or produced other goods for use by the residents of the palace and/or local nobles.

Some evidence suggests that a high proportion of such factory workers were women (some of whom were free and others, slaves). As in all ancient societies, in Mesopotamia women were generally subservient to men. There may have been exceptions to this rule, since information about the lower classes is lacking; and it is possible that women in poor farm households shared equally in the decision-making with their husbands. But in general, women were second-class citizens who were tightly regulated by their husbands and fathers.

This fact of life is reflected in surviving laws. Law number 209 in Hammurabi's code seems designed to protect women: "If a man has struck the daughter of a free man and caused her to cast that which was in her womb [i.e., have a miscarriage], he shall pay ten shekels of silver." Yet law number 210 ensures that an innocent woman will suffer: "If that woman [from the preceding law] died as a result, they shall kill his [the attacker's] daughter."[59] Another law regulating women, this one Assyrian, was discovered by a team

This beatiful ivory head of a well-to-do woman was found in the ruins at Nimrud.

of German archaeologists who excavated the ruins of the city of Assur between 1903 and 1914. "Apart from the penalties for a married woman which are written on the tablet," it reads, "a man may flog his wife, he may pull out her hair, he may damage and split her ears. There is nothing wrong in this."[60] The harsh treatment described here suggests that Assyrian women may have been more abused and subjected to violence than women in other parts of Mesopotamia, although there is no way to know how often such brutal acts were actually carried out.

What little is known for certain about the lives of Mesopotamian women relates to upper-class urban women (who were seen as more respectable than prostitutes and barmaids, who also resided in the cities). Scholar Georges Contenau summarizes the social obligations of a respectable Assyrian daughter/mother:

A DAUGHTER IS SOLD

Most Mesopotamian marriages were arranged, which meant that daughters usually had to marry men chosen by their parents. This surviving Assyrian marriage contract (quoted in Delaporte's *Mesopotamia*), dating from the Sargonid period, suggests that at least some such arrangements involved an exchange of money, in a sense the "sale" of the daughter by her parents.

"Ninlil-hatsina, sister of Nabu-riht-utsur, the lady Nihtes-harau for the price of sixteen shekels of silver has purchased for Tsiha her son for to be his wife; she has taken her away. She is [now] the wife of Tsiha. The money has been paid in full. Whoever in the future at any time at all shall arise and dispute it, be it Nabu-riht-utsur or his children or his grandchildren or his collateral relations or their children or his tutor or anyone that is his, who shall bring a [legal] action or institute proceedings against the lady Nihtes-harau, her children or her grandchildren, that man shall pay ten minae of silver. If he begins the action, he may not profit from it."

Until the time of her marriage a girl remained under the protection of her father, who was free to settle her in marriage exactly as he thought fit. . . . Marriage was preceded by the ceremony of betrothal, during which the girl's future husband poured perfume on her head and brought her presents and provisions. Thereafter the girl was so fully a member of her future husband's family that, if he died, she would marry one of his brothers, or, if he had no brothers, one of his near relatives. The actual marriage . . . took the form of a delivery of the wife to her husband. . . . The ceremony was accompanied by a proper marriage contract, which helped to give the woman the title of wife. If this formality were omitted, cohabitation [living together in the same house] over a period of two years . . . was regarded as the equivalent of a contract. Married life might involve either the wife's staying in her father's house or her going with her husband to his. In the former case, the husband gave the wife a sum called the *dumaki* towards the maintenance of the house, and if the husband died this contribution remained the widow's property only if the deceased had left neither sons nor brothers. . . . If, on the other hand, the young couple went to live in the husband's house, the wife brought with her a *shirqu* . . . or dowry. . . . The *shirqu* . . . remained the inalienable property of her children, and her husband's brothers had no claim on it.[61]

Education

Most women, like most men, were illiterate in ancient Mesopotamia. The relative handful of individuals who possessed the ability to read and write were usually referred to as scribes. From a modern standpoint, the term "scholars" is probably more descriptive, since this small literate class included the ancient equivalents of today's linguists, geographers, physicians, mathematicians, astronomers, and teachers, as well as those who made and copied laws and administrative lists. They attended a special school, called an *edubba*, or "tablet house" (since so much cuneiform writing was done on clay tablets).

That the students who attended these schools almost always came from well-to-do families was proven in the mid–twentieth century by a Luxembourg scholar named Nikolaus Schneider, who carefully examined a huge number of economic and administrative documents dated to about 2000 B.C. Schneider discovered that most of the scribes who wrote and signed these documents also added the names and occupations of their fathers. The fathers were invariably governors, mayors, military officers, priests, high tax officials, temple administrators, scribes, and so on. (In all of these documents, a single woman is listed as a scribe.)

The headmaster of a school was the *ummia* ("school-father"), who was highly respected in the community. In one surviving text, a student (a "school-son") tells his headmaster, "You have opened my eyes as though I were a puppy; you have formed humanity within me."[62] Headmasters were also feared, for discipline was tight and corporal punishment routine in the schools. We know this because of a surviving essay, written about 2000 B.C. by a teacher recalling his own youthful education. Titled "School-days," it tells how the boy's mother gave him his lunch and sent him off to school. But unfortunately for him, he was late. "Afraid and with pounding heart," the boy stood before the headmaster and "made a respectful curtsy," after which the teacher beat him severely with a stick. The essay continues:

> My headmaster read my tablet, [and] said: "There is something missing," [and then he] beat me. The fellow in charge of neatness said: "You loitered in the street and did not straighten up your clothes," [and he also] beat me. The fellow in charge of silence said: "Why did you talk without permission?" [and he also] beat me.[63]

Schools catered to the well-to-do, some of whom are seen here congregating outside a temple.

The beatings went on and on, for every little infraction. Finally, the boy convinced his father to pay the headmaster more money and to invite him over for supper; after that the headmaster warmed up to boy and all was well.

As for the learning that went on in such schools, the fundamental curriculum apparently consisted of mastering languages. In the second and first millennia B.C., these included the prevailing dialects of Akkadian (Babylonian and Assyrian) and of course the literary language of Sumerian. Students learned mainly by rote, repetitively copying lists of words, grammar exercises, letters, poems, and various religious and other kinds of texts. (A large number of tablets containing such student exercises have survived and are on view in museums.) Over time, the pupils also copied math tables and detailed math problems and learned about astronomy, medicine, and other scholarly fields of endeavor.

Making Life More Ordered

Those students who were diligent went on to make important contributions not only to their own society but also to later societies, including many modern ones. This was particularly true in astronomy. The most significant strides in the formative period of this field, which would later become a full-fledged science, were made in Babylonia, long the main cultural model

This clay tablet from the Temple Library at Nippur dates from ca. 2200 B.C. So many cuneiform tablets have been found at Nippur that the city is the primary source of Sumerian literary writings.

for Assyria and other Mesopotamian nations and empires.

Babylonian and other Mesopotamian astronomers were not aloof academics in proverbial ivory towers, remaining out of touch with ordinary people and everyday life. They supplied society with highly practical tools that made life more ordered, the most obvious examples being standardized timekeeping and the calendar. The Babylonian division of the year into twelve lunar months became standard throughout Mesopotamia and in modified form remains in use today across much of the world. "The year began on the first New Moon following the spring equinox," Georges Roux explains,

> and was divided into twelve months of twenty-nine or thirty days. Each day began at sunset and was divided into twelve "double-hours," themselves divided into sixty "double-minutes"—a system which we still follow and owe to the Babylonians. Unfortunately, the lunar year is shorter than the solar year by approximately eleven days, so that after nine years the difference amounts to one full season. . . . For centuries the difficulty created by the difference between the solar year and the lunar year was solved arbitrarily, the king deciding that one or two intercalary [ex-

tra inserted] months should be added to the year [on a periodic basis].[64]

Babylonian and Assyrian astronomers, many of them priests as well as scribes, also provided people with important information about the ways that the heavenly bodies supposedly affected human beings and their lives. To obtain this information (which today is part of the pseudoscience of astrology rather than astronomy), they kept close watch on the heavens, noting the regular movements of the sun, moon, and planets through the twelve constellations of the zodiac. Their instruments were crude by modern standards. These included the gnomon (a rudimentary sundial), the clepsydra (a clock operated by moving water), and the polos (a device that measured the shadow of a tiny ball suspended over a half-sphere).

Through patient, repetitive, and accurate celestial observations, these observers gathered data that they then interpreted in terms of omens and planetary influences on future human events. Mesopotamian kings and their subjects put great store in such predictions, often planning military campaigns and other important undertakings around them; in this way, the fate of whole empires at times rested in the hands of the members of a tiny but very influential educated elite.

CHAPTER SIX

THE DECLINE AND FALL OF THE MESOPOTAMIAN EMPIRES

Like all civilizations and empires, no matter how mighty, those of ancient Mesopotamia eventually declined and disappeared, allowing others to take their place in history's volatile, ever-changing pageant. This did not mean that Mesopotamian beliefs, ideas, and customs died out. To the contrary, the Medes, Persians, and other outside peoples who overran the native Babylonian and Assyrian realms also absorbed many elements of their cultures; and this ensured that Mesopotamian customs and ideas would live on, sometimes in modified forms, for centuries and millennia to come.

The causes for the final decline and collapse of the native Mesopotamian empires are fairly straightforward. In fact, the region had already witnessed a long, repetitive cycle in which local empires had risen and prospered, then declined and fallen. The realm of Sargon of Akkad had been the first large-scale example; it had been followed by the Third Dynasty of Ur, the first Babylonian Empire, several Assyrian realms, and a number of smaller empires and kingdoms. All of these states had gone through periods in which they seemed invincible and permanent. Yet all had been doomed to ultimate failure because their great size and power, so impressive on the surface, had rested on shaky foundations.

An Assyrian soldier leads some Elamite prisoners into exile. War remained an ever-present reality.

Perhaps the most important inherent weakness of these empires was that they were forged through a policy of imperialism. Their blatant, often brutal conquest and subjugation of other peoples was typically followed by attempts to contain, control, and pacify the vanquished. But these attempts failed more often than not, mainly because conquered peoples still harbored both bitterness toward their oppressors and the desire for self-rule. Rebellions were therefore common.

Such insurrections were often aided and strengthened by other weaknesses of the imperial system. One obvious flaw was that some of Mesopotamia's empires became too large for a single centralized administration to govern efficiently. That meant that the king had to allow outlying cities and regions a certain amount of local autonomy; this in turn reinforced the desire for self-rule and opportunity for rebellion in these regions. The inevitable result of all these factors was the decline of the ruling power center and rise of one or more new power centers in its place.

The final decline and fall of ancient Assyria at the hands of the Medes and Babylonians well illustrates this destructive cycle in action. The last great Assyrian empire, especially in its glory years under the Sargonids, had undertaken innumerable campaigns and invasions. It had expended vast amounts of human and material resources, many of which it had looted from those it had conquered. And all the while, it had attempted the gargantuan task of holding together, literally at swordpoint, hundreds of far-flung and frequently rebellious peoples and cities.

The end result was that the Assyrian imperial state had fatally overextended itself. Instead of making friends and alliances among neighbors, the Assyrians had deliberately pursued a policy of war, destruction, and

This fanciful nineteenth-century drawing shows a divine spirit destroying an Assyrian army.

terror, turning these neighbors into bitter enemies. A rebellion by one conquered people might be put down without much fuss; but simultaneous revolts all over the empire strained imperial resources to the breaking point and threatened to topple King Assurbanipal's regime. The Babylonians and Medes, eager to absorb his realm into their own empires, saw their chance and moved in for the kill. Of course, they failed to foresee that they were repeating the same mistakes that the Assyrians had and that they would soon suffer the same calamitous fate.

The Fall of Nimrud and Nineveh

Despite its many centuries of imperial greatness, once Assyria's enemies began to close

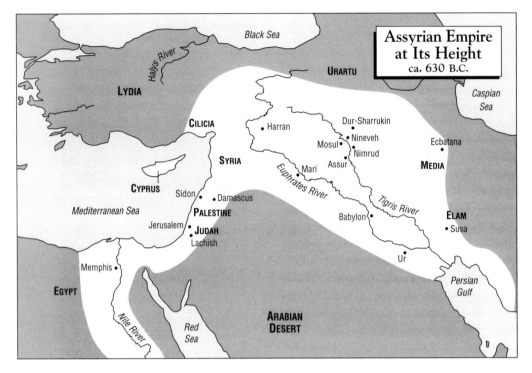

in, its collapse was frighteningly swift and permanent. The Median king Cyaxares, who had been building a large and formidable army and expanding his realm in what is now southern Iran, heard the reports of rebellions in many Assyrian provinces. He also learned that Babylonia's king Nabopolassar had begun a major offensive against Assyria. The time seemed ripe and Cyaxares swiftly prepared for his own assault on the tottering Assyrian colossus.

In 615 B.C., less than a year after the Babylonians attacked Assyria, Cyaxares' forces suddenly swept out of the Zagros foothills and took the town of Arrapha, about sixty miles east of Assur. Meeting surprisingly little resistance, the Medes followed up the following year with an audacious attack on Assur itself, the oldest and most sacred of Assyria's cities. Hearing of the Medes' march on Assur, Nabopolassar rushed his

troops to the scene, hoping to take part in the attack and share in the victory spoils; but he arrived too late. Nevertheless, he and Cyaxares both saw the wisdom of an alliance against their mutual foe. There, in Assur's ruins, they signed a pact and soon afterward sealed it by bringing together in marriage Nabopolassar's son, Nebuchadrezzar, and the Median princess Amytis.

Perhaps by applying all of its remaining resources in an all-out effort, Assyria might have been able to hold its own against either the Babylonians or the Medes acting alone. Confronted with the alliance between these formidable opponents, however, the Assyrian Empire was doomed. In the summer of 612 B.C., Nabopolassar's and Cyaxares' forces poured into the Assyrian heartland north of Assur, taking town after town. Reaching Nimrud, they stormed its protective fort, which had come to be used as a storehouse for valuable treasures and writing tablets.

Austen Henry Layard had noted some of the evidence for Nimrud's destruction in the late 1840s in his classic excavations of this city. But the full extent of the damage did not come to light until the work of an expedition mounted by the British School of Archeology between 1949 and 1960. Led by English scholar M. E. L. Mallowen, the excavators dug around the base of the walls of the large fort that guarded the city; there, in 1958, they found many spearheads and other fragments of weapons, evidence of the desperate, bloody fighting that raged as the Babylonian and Median attackers swarmed over the battlements. These and other artifacts were carefully sketched and photographed in their original positions, or *in situ*. This is done partly to give scholars an accurate picture of how the site's individual elements are related to one another, thus establishing whether they are from the same or different chronological time periods. For example, artifacts found in deeper layers are usually (though not always) older than those found above them. Eventually, excavators remove the more delicate artifacts and take them to museums for preservation and study.

As the dig at Nimrud's ruined fort continued, the archaeologists concentrated on the structure's central storeroom. Here, they found a six-foot-thick ash layer, attesting to the severity of the fire the victors lit as they viciously laid waste to the once great city. "In these ashes," writes Danish Mesopotamian scholar Jorgen Laessoe,

In the 1950s, an expedition mounted by the British School of Archaeology found widespread evidence of an all-out attack on the defenses of Nimrud, whose ruins are seen here.

ESARHADDON'S TREATY WITH MEDIA

Before Media's rise to greatness, the Assyrian king Esarhaddon concluded a treaty with the Medes designed to cement Assyria's domination over them. These excerpts from the treaty were discovered in the ruins of Nimrud, while copies of other similar treaties were broken or burned by the Median troops who sacked Nimrud in 612 B.C.

"This is the treaty that Esarhaddon, king of the world, king of Assyria, son of Sennacherib, he who was likewise king of the world . . . concludes with Ramataia, prince of the city of Urakazabarna [in Media], with his sons, his grandsons, with all the people of [his] realm, young and old, as many as there are. . . . In the presence of the planets Jupiter, Venus, Saturn, Mercury, Mars, [the star] Sirius, and in the presence of Assur, Anu, Enlil, Ea, Sin, [and other great gods] . . . this is the treaty that Esarhaddon, king of Assyria, has concluded with you in the presence of the great gods of heaven and earth concerning Assurbanipal, the crown prince, son of your lord Esarhaddon, who he has named and appointed as crown prince. When Esarhaddon . . . dies. . . he [Assurbanipal] will exercise the kingship and sovereignty of Assyria over you. You shall protect him in town and country: you shall fight and die for him. With the truth of your heart shall you talk with him. You shall counsel him with loyal mind. You shall clear a good road for him. You swear that you shall not be hostile to him . . . that you will not transgress against him; that you will not lift a hand against him for evil intent; that you will not rise against him or undertake anything against him that is not good and seemly. . . . You swear that you will not alter this treaty, that you will not consign it to the fire, or cast it into the water . . . or destroy it in any deliberate manner. . . . If you do so . . . let [the god] Sin . . . invest you with leprosy . . . let [the god] Ninurta . . . strike you down with his swift arrow; let him fill the steppe with your bodies; let him give your flesh as meat to eagle and jackal."

lay hundreds of broken and blackened pieces of the Assyrian kings' collection of gold-plated ivories. . . . Copies of the . . . treaties concluded by [Assyrian king] Esarhadden with Median princes sixty years earlier . . . were all smashed into hundreds of fragments. Is it possible that this fact betokens [signifies] the long awaited vengeance of the Medes on this city which contained the most disgraceful documents in their history?[65]

The merciless wave of destruction that had engulfed Nimrud and other cities finally reached the gates of Assyria's largest and most important metropolis—Nineveh. A month or two later, in faraway Palestine, the Hebrew prophet Nahum penned this vivid description of the city's end:

> The shatterer [Cyaxares? Nabopolassar? the hand of God?] has come up against you. Man the ramparts . . . collect all your strength . . . . The shield of his mighty men is red, his soldiers are clothed in scarlet. The chariots flash like flame when mustered in array; the chargers prance. The chariots rage in the streets, they rush to and fro through the squares; they gleam like torches, they dart like lightning. . . . The river gates are opened, the palace is in dismay; its mistress [the queen?] is stripped, she is carried off, her maidens lamenting. . . . Nineveh is like a pool whose waters run away. "Halt! Halt!" they cry; but none turns back. Plunder the silver, plunder the gold! There is no end of treasure, or wealth of every precious thing. Desolate! Desolation and ruin! Hearts faint and knees tremble, anguish is on all loins, all faces grow pale![66]

An Epitaph for the Assyrians

Though the invaders had converted the main Assyrian cities to smoldering heaps of rubble, their task was not yet finished. One of King Assurbanipal's sons, Sin-shar-ishkun, perished somehow, perhaps at the hands of his own officers; and one of these officers now claimed the throne. He took the name of King Assuruballit, who some seven hundred years before had launched Assyria's first great empire by seizing large sections of the Near East.

This new, much less formidable Assuruballit hastily scraped together the few Assyrian troops who had survived the capture of the nation's heartland, fled westward, and made a last stand at Harran, on the upper reaches of the Euphrates. There he was reinforced by a regiment of Egyptian troops, who had finally arrived in fulfillment of an Assyrian-Egyptian alliance concluded about four years prior. In 610 B.C., according to a Babylonian chronicle, the Medes and Babylonians, encouraged by their prior victories, advanced on Harran:

> In the sixteenth year [of Nabopolassar's reign] . . . the king of Akkad mobilized his army and . . . [the Medes] came to the support of Akkad and they united their armies and toward Harran, against Assuruballit, who sat on the throne in Assyria, they marched. Assuruballit and the army of Kullania [likely the Egyptian commander], which had come to his aid—fear of the enemy fell upon them and they forsook the city.[67]

The chronicle suggests that not long after fleeing, Assuruballit returned and attempted to retake Harran, but that he was unsuccessful. And thereafter, he, the throne, and what little was left of the Assyrian government were simply heard of no more.

The brief but fearsome Babylonian-Median campaign was so shattering that Assyria's heartland, which had remained continuously inhabited and prosperous for almost two thousand years, lay devastated; the last remnants of the once huge and mighty empire ruled from that heartland quickly fell to pieces; and in the decades and centuries that followed, all that remained of that realm was the memory of its cruelty to its conquered subjects. Babylonia's Nabopolassar himself made reference to the fear and damage Assyria had so long wrought throughout the Near East in a statement that could be taken as an epitaph for the fallen masters of Assur:

> I slaughtered the land of Assyria, I turned the hostile land into heaps and ruins. The Assyrian, who since distant days had ruled over all the peoples and with his heavy yoke had brought injury to the people of the Land [i.e., Babylonia], their feet from Akkad I turned back; their yoke I threw off.[68]

As for the Assyrian people, those who managed to survive the fall of their country must have eked out whatever livings they could in the shadows of their new masters and wondered why the great god Assur had abandoned them. As the years passed, their children and their children's children were largely absorbed into the Near East's ever-churning melting pot of peoples, although small groups of people kept alive the Assyrian language; and their distant descendants, still identifying themselves as Assyrians, can be found in Iraq and other parts of the Near East today.

Babylonia's Troubles Begin

The annihilation of the Assyrian Empire near the close of the seventh century B.C. marked the beginning of the end of native

An eighteenth-century illustration portrays the Hebrew king Ahab battling the Assyrians. In 853 B.C., he joined with other local Palestinian rulers in repelling an Assyrian invasion.

Mesopotamian power in the Near East. It also created a new balance of power in that region, in which four nations of roughly the same strength dominated various areas. Cyaxares' Media controlled southern and western Iran and parts of northern Mesopotamia; Nabopolassar's Neo-Babylonia held sway over the rest of Mesopotamia and claimed sovereignty over some of the former Assyrian vassals in Palestine and Syria; Egypt also had designs on Palestine and Syria; and Lydia, a relatively new but rich and powerful kingdom, dominated western and central Anatolia. These nations were not content with the status quo, and inevitably disputes and wars erupted among them. Thus, the last Assyrian kings were not yet cold in their graves, so to speak, when the Near East entered a new cycle of ambition, bloody conquest, and the rise and fall of empires.

The first major face-off in the post-Assyrian political landscape was between Babylonia and Egypt over control of the Mediterranean coast. The Egyptians, who had recently moved troops north in a vain attempt to help the last Assyrian ruler, now controlled Syria as far north as Carchemish. Nabopolassar delegated the task of dislodging the Egyptians from that key city to his son Nebuchadrezzar, who did so in 605 B.C. Nebuchadrezzar then marched south through Palestine, demanding vassal allegiance from Judah and other states. He had nearly reached Pelusium, on Egypt's border, when the news arrived that his father, Nabopolassar, had died. The son hastened to Babylon, where he eagerly took charge of his father's crown and growing empire.

But to the new king's dismay, the newly expansionist Babylonia now began to experience some of the same troubles Assyria had in trying to hold together an empire of far-flung and diverse peoples. In the next few years, several

Babylonia's king Nebuchadrezzar is triumphant over the Hebrew city of Jerusalem in 587 B.C.

Palestinian states, including Judah, rebelled. And Nebuchadrezzar, though he had grown up hating the Assyrians for their cruelty, now used some of the same tactics they had, including acts of terror and the deportation of city populations to distant and/or remote areas. Roberta L. Harris tells of Judah's fate after the Babylonians captured Jerusalem in 587 B.C.:

> The Babylonians first looted Jerusalem, destroying the Temple, and then set the city on fire. . . . Zedekiah [the Judaean ruler] fled the city but was captured and brought before Nebuchadrezzar at Riblah in Syria. He was forced to witness the execution of his sons, was then blinded and taken to Babylon in chains. Many of the important citizens of Jerusalem were sent after their king

HERODOTUS ON THE RISE OF MEDIA

In his famous *Histories*, the fifth-century B.C. Greek historian Herodotus gives the following account of the efforts of the rulers Deioces and Phraortes to unify the Median tribes. Herodotus ends with the introduction of the Persians, who would eventually overcome and absorb the Medes, Babylonians, and many other Near Eastern peoples.

"The Medes had established themselves in small settlements, and Deioces, who was already a man of mark in his own village, now entered wholeheartedly into the task of distinguishing himself for just dealing. In this he had a purpose; for throughout the country at that time there was no sort of organized government whatever. . . . Bent upon getting all power into his own hands, he performed this office with perfect integrity. . . . Once the news of Deioces' integrity got abroad, everyone was glad to submit cases to his judgment. . . . [After rising in prestige and power until he became king of all the Medes, Deioces] continued his strict administration of justice. . . . The achievement of Deioces, who reigned for fifty years, was to unite under his rule the people of Media—Busae, Parataceni, Struchates, Arazanti, Budii, Magi; beyond these he did not extend his empire. His son Phraortes, however, who succeeded to the throne on his father's death, was not content to be king only of Media; he carried his military operations further afield, and the first country he attacked and brought into subjection was Persia [in the region of Fārs, in southern Iran]."

into exile. . . . Whole families must have packed up their belongings on ox-carts, to make the terrible journey of several hundred miles to a strange new land.[69]

The Eclipse of Babylonia and Media

Meanwhile, many miles to the north and east, the Medes were involved in their own program of conquest and expansion. Not long after consolidating the former northern Assyrian lands, Cyaxares' armies were once more on the march. And by 590 B.C. they had captured much of Armenia, the mountainous region lying east of Anatolia. By this act, the Medians showed that they had not paid heed to the lessons of the past; for Assyria had earlier invested, and in the long run wasted, many precious human and material resources in their campaigns in Armenia.

Convinced that these aggressions had made him stronger, Cyaxares, like Nebuchadrezzar, apparently did not foresee the serious problems he faced in maintaining a vast empire of discontented vassals. So in 589 B.C. the overconfident Median ruler moved farther westward and brazenly invaded the newest of the Near Eastern great powers, Lydia. The Lydian king Alyattes met the challenge with his own formidable army and, according to Herodotus, the war "continued for five years during which both Lydians and Medes won a number of victories."[70]

Ironically, it was natural, rather than human, forces that brought the Median-Lydian war to a sudden and unexpected halt. In one of history's greatest accidents of timing, on May 28, 585 B.C., at the height of a great battle between the opposing forces, a total eclipse of the sun occurred. Herodotus later recorded: "After five years of indecisive warfare, a battle took place in which the armies had already engaged, when day was suddenly turned into night. . . . Both Lydians and Medes broke off the engagement when they saw this darkening of the day."[71] Believing the eclipse to be an omen of ill fortune, the Medes marched out of Lydia, never to return.

Cyaxares died the following year, unaware that the eclipse would indeed prove a portent of bad luck for the Medes; for their short-lived empire was itself soon eclipsed by one of their own subject peoples—the Persians. Hailing from the small region of Fārs, in southern Iran, the Persians and their ancestors had witnessed the long and relentless rise and fall of empires in other parts of the Near East. Now it was their turn to enter that repetitive cycle of *construction* and *destruction*.

Beginning in the 550s B.C., a brilliant, charismatic, and talented Persian nobleman,

Persia's Cyrus the Great enters Babylon in 539 B.C. after encountering little resistance from the natives. The city subsequently became one of his realm's three capitals.

Cyrus II, led a successful rebellion that quickly toppled the short-lived Median Empire and then went on to conquer, in rapid succession, Lydia, Babylonia, and parts of Palestine. At its greatest extent, under some of Cyrus's successors, the Persian realm became the greatest empire the world had yet seen. This vast dominion, stretching from northern Greece in the west to the borders of India in the east, and from Egypt in the south to central Armenia in the north, contained literally hundreds of different peoples, ethnic groups, and languages. In the years to come, the Persian Empire, like the great Mesopotamian empires it supplanted, would accomplish great deeds, spread its culture far and wide, and appear to be invincible. But also like them, it was doomed to go the way of all human empires. To it too could be applied the haunting epitaph written by the Hebrew prophet Zephaniah for the once mighty city of Nineveh:

> This is the exultant city that dwelt secure, that said to herself, "I am and there is none else." What a desolation she had become, a lair for wild beasts! Everyone who passes by her hisses and shakes his fist.[72]

MESOPOTAMIA'S LIVING LEGACY

The old adage that "history repeats itself" may by now sound tired and overused. It is, nonetheless, often quite true. The long, turbulent history of the Near East following the decline and fall of the native Mesopotamian empires is a case in point. The vast Persian Empire, which overcame the last of these once great realms, enjoyed a period of wealth and power, but then, like them, fell apart from a combination of internal problems and external threats.

The destructive cycle of rising and falling empires then continued apace. The Macedonian (Greek) Alexander the Great, who had conquered Persia between 334 and 323 B.C., incorporated its lands into his own empire. But

Macedonia's young but gifted king, Alexander III, whom posterity came to call "the Great," occupies one of Persia's capitals after defeating the last of its kings, Darius III.

this vast new Macedonian realm barely out-lived its creator. Not long after Alexander's passing, his leading generals (the so-called "Successors") fell into a power struggle over who should succeed him. These ambitious men waged a series of devastating wars that lasted over forty years. Finally, by about 280 B.C., three large kingdoms emerged in what had been Alexander's empire; the biggest, founded by Seleucus, encompassed the former Assyrian, Babylonian, Median, and Persian homelands, along with sections of Palestine and Anatolia. In time, the Seleucid realm also crumbled, giv-ing way to the Parthian Empire (ca. 140 B.C.), which in turn was absorbed by the Sassanian Empire (in A.D. 224), which itself fell to Is-lamic Arab armies (ca. 650).

The Driving Force of History

And so it continued—one conquest following another, with a constant infusion of new peo-ples, cultures, and beliefs, each merging with the older, traditional ones to form the highly diversified hybrid cultures of the modern Near East. These cultural survivals constitute the lasting legacy of the ancient Mesopotamian empires. In a sense, says Daniel Snell, these realms died out only in the political sense, while important elements of their cultures lived on. "The texts that documented them ceased," he writes, "their rulers changed, and they became slowly the societies and economies of the region today."[73]

The essence and influence of these an-cient societies does indeed live on. They are evident not only in the rich Near Eastern cultural mix that they helped to shape in profound ways, but also in the many crucial contributions they made to world culture, beginning with the creation of the first cities. As Michael Wood aptly and mov-ingly puts it:

> The Mesopotamians conceived of civilization as separate from nature, set in an artificial environment of man's creation [the city], which could insulate human society from the threats of primal nature. . . . Mesopotamian city civilization then represents a dramatic break with the cultural continuum of the prehistoric world which had lasted for tens of thousands of years. . . . It was only the Near East which made this leap for-ward: in technology; in large-scale trade; in irrigation; in the use of writ-ing for economic purposes . . . in the cosmological evolution which sepa-rated gods from nature. Why this hap-pened only in the Near East towards 3000 B.C. is one of the great questions of history. For these ideas were trans-mitted to the later civilizations of the West, developed there and became enshrined as universal experience by the West in the last three centuries. Coupled with [Western] ideas of indi-vidual freedom, these are now seen as the driving force of history.[74]

Notes

Introduction: The Cradle of the Human Race?

1. Quoted in Michael Wood, *Legacy: The Search for Ancient Cultures*. New York: Sterling Publishing, 1992, p. 10.
2. Quoted in C. W. Ceram, *The March of Archaeology*, trans. Richard and Clara Winston. New York: Knopf, 1958, p. 198.
3. Quoted in Wood, *Legacy*, pp. 11–12.
4. A. Leo Oppenheim, *Ancient Mesopotamia: Portrait of a Dead Civilization*. Chicago: University of Chicago Press, 1977, pp. 7–9.

Chapter One: Mesopotamia's Early Peoples and First Cities

5. Quoted in C. W. Ceram, *Gods, Graves, and Scholars: The Story of Archaeology*, trans. E. B. Garside and Sophie Wilkins. New York: Random House, 1986, p. 286.
6. A. Leo Oppenheim, *Letters from Mesopotamia: Official, Business, and Private Letters on Clay Tablets from Two Millennia*. Chicago: University of Chicago Press, 1967, pp. 2–3.
7. Wood, *Legacy*, pp. 18–19.
8. Daniel C. Snell, *Life in the Ancient Near East*, 3100–332 B.C. New Haven: Yale University Press, 1997, p. 12.

9. Trevor Watkins, "The Beginnings of Warfare," in Sir John Hackett, ed., *Warfare in the Ancient World*. New York: Facts On File, 1989, p. 16.
10. Snell, *Life in the Ancient Near East*, p. 14.
11. Some scholars suggest that the Sumerian language may be remotely related to the Dravidian languages of India, which are themselves related to Elamite, the early language of southern Iran, the region adjacent to eastern Sumer. For an enlightening overview of the various arguments about Sumerian origins, see Tom B. Jones, ed., *The Sumerian Problem*. New York: John Wiley, 1969.
12. H. W. F. Saggs, *Civilization Before Greece and Rome*. New Haven: Yale University Press, 1989, p. 45.
13. Wood, *Legacy*, p. 27.
14. Samuel N. Kramer, *Cradle of Civilization*. New York: Time-Life, 1967, p. 35.

Chapter Two: The Great Age of Mesopotamian Empires

15. Saggs, *Civilization Before Greece and Rome*, p. 41.
16. Watkins, "Beginnings of Warfare," in Hackett, ed., *Warfare in the Ancient World*, p. 19.

17. Georges Roux, *Ancient Iraq.* New York: Penguin, 1980, p. 140.

18. James Henry Breasted, *Ancient Times: A History of the Early World.* Boston: Ginn and Company, 1944, p. 180.

19. Quoted in Jorgen Laessoe, *People of Ancient Assyria: Their Inscriptions and Correspondence,* trans. F. S. Leigh-Browne. London: Routledge and Kegan Paul, 1963, p. 43.

20. Quoted in Daniel D. Luckenbill, ed., *Ancient Records of Assyria and Babylonia.* 2 vols. Chicago: University of Chicago Press, 1926. Reprint, New York: Greenwood Press, 1968, vol. 1, p. 17.

21. Quoted in Luckenbill, *Ancient Records of Assyria and Babylonia,* vol. 1, p. 51.

22. Historians have advanced a number of theories to explain this widespread catastrophe. Some think that rapid local population growth among the semibarbarous tribes inhabiting the vast steppe lands north of the Black and Caspian Seas caused them to migrate southward in search of new lands, destroying all in their path. Others suggest that climatic factors, such as a prolonged dry spell, caused these mass migrations. Another theory holds that a large portion of the destruction was caused by civil conflicts, economic collapse, and other crises within the Near Eastern states themselves. And still another view, advanced recently by Robert Drews of Vanderbilt University, is that military innovations among the "periphery" peoples living near the borders of these kingdoms suddenly gave their foot soldiers the ability to defeat the chariot corps that had for centuries been the mainstay of Near Eastern armies. For a detailed discussion, see Robert Drews, *The End of the Bronze Age: Changes in Warfare and the Catastrophe ca. 1200 B.C.* Princeton: Princeton University Press, 1993.

23. Roberta L. Harris, *The World of the Bible.* London: Thames and Hudson, 1995, p. 93.

24. Quoted in Luckenbill, *Ancient Records of Assyria and Babylonia,* vol. 2, p. 417.

Chapter Three: High Culture and Art in Ancient Mesopotamia

25. Saggs, *Civilization Before Greece and Rome,* pp. 6–7.

26. Quoted in Kramer, *Cradle of Civilization,* p. 127.

27. Quoted in Kramer, *Cradle of Civilization,* p. 128.

28. Snell, *Life in the Ancient Near East,* p. 18.

29. Quoted in C. W. Ceram, ed., *Hands on the Past: Pioneer Archaeologists Tell Their Own Story.* New York: Knopf, 1966, p. 250.

30. Quoted in Morris Jastrow, *The Civilizations of Babylonia and Assyria.* Philadelphia: J. B. Lippincott, 1915, pp. 448–50.

31. Roux, *Ancient Iraq,* pp. 90–91.

32. Roux, *Ancient Iraq,* p. 92.

33. Chester G. Starr, *A History of the*

Ancient World. New York: Oxford University Press, 1991, p. 135.

34. Quoted in Ceram, *Hands on the Past*, pp. 241–42.

35. Herodotus, *The Histories*, trans. Aubrey de Sélincourt. New York: Penguin, 1972, p. 113.

36. Herodotus, *Histories*, p. 114.

37. Quoted in Peter Clayton and Martin Price, *The Seven Wonders of the Ancient World*. New York: Barnes and Noble, 1993, pp. 43–44.

38. Quoted in Ceram, *Hands on the Past*, p. 232.

Chapter Four: Of Peasants and Kings: Mesopotamian Social Organization

39. Oppenheim, *Ancient Mesopotamia*, p. 65.

40. Roux, *Ancient Iraq*, p. 312.

41. Oppenheim, *Ancient Mesopotamia*, p. 100.

42. Quoted in Luckenbill, *Ancient Records of Assyria and Babylonia*, vol. 2, p. 379.

43. Saggs, *Civilization Before Greece and Rome*, p. 36.

44. Kramer, *Cradle of Civilization*, p. 81.

45. Quoted in Kramer, *Cradle of Civilization*, p. 68.

46. Oppenheim, *Ancient Mesopotamia*, p. 108.

47. Snell, *Life in the Ancient Near East*, p. 122.

48. Snell, *Life in the Ancient Near East*, p. 123.

49. Snell, *Life in the Ancient Near East*, pp. 122–24.

50. Saggs, *Civilization Before Greece and Rome*, p. 126.

51. Saggs, *Civilization Before Greece and Rome*, p. 44.

Chapter Five: Aspects of Everyday Life in Ancient Mesopotamia

52. Quoted in Kramer, *Cradle of Civilization*, p. 127.

53. Kramer, *Cradle of Civilization*, p. 87.

54. For an excellent, informative, and very readable discussion of building materials, tools, and methods and how they were used in houses, palaces, temples, canals, and more, see L. Sprague de Camp, *The Ancient Engineers*. New York: Ballantine Books, 1963, specifically, "The Mesopotamian Engineers," pp. 46–82.

55. Quoted in Samuel N. Kramer, *The Sumerians: Their History, Culture and Character*. Chicago: University of Chicago Press, 1971, pp. 340–41.

56. Quoted in Kramer, *Cradle of Civilization*, p. 79.

57. Kramer, *Cradle of Civilization*, p. 85.

58. Saggs, *Civilization Before Greece and Rome*, p. 124.

59. Quoted in Saggs, *Civilization Before Greece and Rome*, p. 159.

60. Quoted in Saggs, *Civilization Before Greece and Rome*, p. 169.

61. Georges Contenau, *Everyday Life in Babylon and Assyria*. London: Edward Arnold, 1964, pp. 15–17.

62. Quoted in Saggs, *Civilization Before Greece and Rome*, p. 105.

63. Quoted in Kramer, *The Sumerians,* p. 238.
64. Roux, *Ancient Iraq,* pp. 336–37.

Chapter Six: The Decline and Fall of the Mesopotamian Empires
65. Laessoe, *People of Ancient Assyria,* p. 124.
66. Nahum 2:1–10, in the Bible.
67. Quoted in Luckenbill, *Ancient Records of Assyria and Babylonia,* vol. 2, pp. 420–21.

68. Quoted in A. T. Olmstead, *History of Assyria.* Chicago: University of Chicago Press, 1923, 1960, 1968, p. 640.
69. Harris, *World of the Bible,* p. 97.
70. Herodotus, *Histories,* p. 70.
71. Herodotus, *Histories,* p. 71.
72. Zephaniah 2:13–15, in the Bible.

Epilogue: Mesopotamia's Living Legacy
73. Snell, *Life in the Ancient Near East,* p. 143.
74. Wood, *Legacy,* pp. 48–49.

Chronology

B.C.

ca. 5500

People from the upland areas surrounding the Mesopotamian plains begin to descend from the hills and settle in the Tigris and Euphrates River valleys.

ca. 3300–3000

The Sumerians build the first Mesopotamian cities, in the plain just northwest of the Persian Gulf; the Sumerians also begin using a complex writing system that evolves into what modern scholars call cuneiform.

ca. 2400–2200

Akkadian rulers, most prominent among them King Sargon, conquer Sumeria and unite northern and southern Mesopotamia.

ca. 2100

Ur-Nammu, king of the city of Ur, establishes a new empire, the Third Dynasty of Ur.

ca. 2000

An unknown Babylonian scribe collects the epic tales of the early Mesopotamian hero Gilgamesh; the Sumerian language has by now ceased to be widely spoken and is used only by priests and scholars.

ca. 1813–1781

Reign of Shamshi-Adad, founder of Assyria's first great royal dynasty and the first of that nation's rulers about whom any details are known.

ca. 1759

Babylonian king Hammurabi conquers the kingdom of Mari, on the upper Euphrates, and soon afterward absorbs Assur and the other Assyrian cities.

ca. 1600
Babylon is sacked by the Hittites, an ambitious people from central Anatolia (Asia Minor).

ca. 1365–1330
Reign of Assuruballit I, first king of the newly independent Assyria.

ca. 1200
Many Near Eastern and Mediterranean cities are sacked and burned, including those of the Hittites, as the region undergoes catastrophic upheaval, the causes of which remain unclear; Assyria largely escapes the destruction, leaving it the lone surviving great power in the western Near Eastern sphere.

ca. 744–727
Reign of Tiglathpileser III, who reasserts Assyrian domination of Syria and Palestine, taking Damascus and annexing half of Israel.

ca. 722–705
Reign of Sargon II, founder of the Sargonid dynasty, who crushes numerous rebellions and builds a new royal palace at Dur-Sharrukin (Khorsabad), northeast of Nineveh.

ca. 694
Sargon's successor, Sennacherib, destroys Babylon.

ca. 681
Sennacherib is assassinated by his own sons; one of them, Esarhaddon, ascends the throne and soon begins rebuilding Babylon.

ca. 668–627
Reign of Assurbanipal, who inherits the Assyrian Empire at its height of power.

627
Assurbanipal dies and Assyria is wracked by rebellions and civil war.

626
Chaldean ruler Nabopolassar seizes Babylon and launches a war against the weakened Assyria.

615

Media's King Cyaxares attacks Assyria from the east; the following year he captures and sacks Assur, the most sacred of Assyria's cities; Cyaxares and Nabopolassar form an anti-Assyrian alliance.

612

A combined Babylonian-Median army ravages the Assyrian heartland, destroying Nimrud and Nineveh.

589

Cyaxares invades the kingdom of Lydia, in central Anatolia.

558

Cyrus the Great rises to the throne of Persia, a small kingdom of southern Iran that was then a subject of Media.

539

Having conquered and absorbed Media, Cyrus captures the great Mesopotamian city of Babylon.

334–323

Macedonian conqueror Alexander the Great subdues the mighty Persian Empire.

ca. 140

The Parthian Empire rises in the region once occupied by the great Mesopotamian empires.

A.D.

ca. 650

Islamic Arab armies conquer much of the Near East, including what was once Mesopotamia and is now Iraq.

1845–1851

British-sponsored archaeologist Austen Henry Layard excavates the Assyrian capitals of Nimrud and Nineveh, making numerous important discoveries, including magnificent carved bas-reliefs depicting the exploits of Assyria's kings.

1849

English linguist Henry C. Rawlinson makes great strides in the decipherment of the ancient Mesopotamian writing system, called cuneiform.

1872

English scholar and archaeologist George Smith translates the Mesopotamian epic tale of the hero Gilgamesh, which had a profound affect on the literatures of later ancient cultures.

1902

A team of French archaeologists discovers a tablet bearing the famous law code of the Babylonian king Hammurabi.

1914

Having led a large team of diggers at the site of Babylon for several years, German archaeologist Robert Koldewey publishes his *Excavations at Babylon*.

1958

British archaeologists find widespread evidence for the ultimate defeat and destruction of a Mesopotamian empire in the ruins of the Assyrian city of Nimrud.

FOR FURTHER READING

Michael W. Davison, ed., *Everyday Life Through the Ages*. London: Reader's Digest Association, 1992. This large, beautifully illustrated volume, which examines the way people lived in various cultures throughout history, has a section on ancient Assyria, as well as sections on ancient Babylonia, Persia, and Greece.

Samuel N. Kramer, *Cradle of Civilization*. New York: Time Inc., 1967. Written by one of the world's foremost scholars of Mesopotamian culture and lavishly illustrated with stunning photos and drawings, this remains one of the very best basic presentations of Mesopotamian civilization for general readers.

Hazel M. Martell, *The Ancient World: From the Ice Age to the Fall of Rome*. New York: Kingfisher, 1995. A very handsomely mounted book that briefly examines the various important ancient civilizations, including many of those mentioned in this volume about ancient Assyria.

Don Nardo, *The Persian Empire*. San Diego: Lucent Books, 1997. This is in a sense the sequel to the present volume about Mesopotamia; it begins with the destruction of Nineveh and other important Assyrian cities by the Babylonians and Medes and then chronicles the rise and two-century-long reign of the Persians, who based many of their military and administrative customs on earlier Mesopotamian models.

Chester G. Starr, *Early Man: Prehistory and the Civilizations of the Ancient Near East*. New York: Oxford University Press, 1973. A very well-organized and useful general overview of the pageant of Near Eastern peoples, from the first hunter-gatherers through the Sumerians, Babylonians, Egyptians, Assyrians, and Persians, told by a world-class historian.

Tim Wood, *Ancient Wonders*. New York: Penguin Books, 1991. This beautifully illustrated and informative volume examines the most famous buildings and monuments of ancient times, including the Hanging Gardens of Babylon, built by the son of the Babylonian ruler who destroyed the Assyrian Empire once and for all.

WORKS CONSULTED

Major Sources:

Jean Bottéro, *Mesopotamia: Writing, Reasoning, and the Gods*. Trans. Zainab Bahrani and Marc Van De Mieroop. Chicago: University of Chicago Press, 1992. A thorough and well-written account of ancient Mesopotamian writing, thought, and religion. Will appeal mainly to scholars and serious students of the ancient Near East.

C. W. Ceram, ed., *Hands on the Past: Pioneer Archaeologists Tell Their Own Story*. New York: Knopf, 1966. This extremely informative and valuable book is a collection of firsthand accounts by the great excavators. Highly recommended for those interested in past cultures.

C. W. Ceram, *The March of Archaeology*. Trans. Richard and Clara Winston. New York: Knopf, 1958. An excellent general synopsis of the first century and a half of archaeological endeavors around the world, including the exploits of Niebuhr, Rich, Botta, Layard, Rawlinson, Koldewey, and others in Mesopotamia.

Georges Contenau, *Everyday Life in Babylon and Assyria*. London: Edward Arnold, 1964. Contenau, a distinguished Assyriologist, here concentrates on the period of circa 700 to 530 B.C., encompassing Assyria and Babylonia at their heights, partly because it is representative of these cultures and also because it is their most documented period. He covers diverse aspects of society, including home life, marriage, farming, trade, religion, literature, entertainment, and much more.

Sir John Hackett, ed., *Warfare in the Ancient World*. New York: Facts On File, 1989. This extremely informative and handsome volume is a collection of long, detailed essays by world-class historians, each of whom tackles the military development and methods of a single ancient people or empire. The beautiful and accurate illustrations are by the famous scholar-artist Peter Connolly. Of main interest for the purposes of this volume on Mesopotamia are "The Beginnings of Warfare" (pp. 15–35), by Dr. Trevor Watkins, of the Archeology Deparment at Edinburgh University, who summarizes the weapons and tactics of the Sumerians and other early Near Eastern peoples; and "The Assyrians" (pp. 36–53), by D. J. Wiseman, the distinguished Assyriologist of the University of London who examines in detail the fearsome military machine that terrorized the Near East and significantly influenced the later Persian military.

Holy Bible. Revised Standard Version. New York: Thomas Nelson and Sons, 1952. The Bible contains numerous references to the Assyrians, Babylonians, and other Near Eastern peoples with whom they interacted. Although not straightforward historical chronicles, these tracts preserve valuable information about people, customs, and events of the Near East in the first millennium B.C., data that historians attempt to correlate with Assyrian and Babylonian chronicles and archaeological finds.

Samuel N. Kramer, *The Sumerians: Their History, Culture and Character*. Chicago: University of Chicago Press, 1971. An invaluable source of information about early Mesopotamia, including a great deal of primary source material, clearly written by one of the great twentieth-century experts in the field. Highly recommended.

Jorgen Laessoe, *People of Ancient Assyria: Their Inscriptions and Correspondence*. Trans. F. S. Leigh-Browne. London: Routledge and Kegan Paul, 1963. This worthwhile overview of Assyrian history is supported by numerous long primary source quotes.

Austen Henry Layard, *Nineveh and Its Remains*. 2 vols. London: John Murray, 1867. The important and fascinating discoveries made by one of the greatest excavators of the nineteenth century are described in detail in this summary, a classic in the field of archaeology, that he originally published in 1849.

Daniel D. Luckenbill, ed., *Ancient Records of Assyria and Babylonia*. 2 vols. Chicago: University of Chicago Press, 1926. Reprint, New York: Greenwood Press, 1968. This set is among a handful of major compilations of English translations of ancient Assyrian and Babylonian annals, letters, inscriptions, and other documents routinely consulted and quoted by scholars and serious students of Mesopotamian civilization. Among the others I have used in writing this book are A. Leo Oppenheim's *Letters from Mesopotamia: Official, Business, and Private Letters on Clay Tablets from Two Millennia.* Chicago: University of Chicago Press, 1967; and Leroy Waterman's *Royal Correspondence of the Assyrian Empire.* 4 vols. Ann Arbor: University of Michigan Press, 1930–36.

A. T. Olmstead, *History of Assyria.* Chicago: University of Chicago Press, 1923, 1960, 1968. This massive (655 pages) and authoritative volume by the late Professor Olmstead, one of the preeminent Near Eastern scholars of the first half of the twentieth century, is now somewhat dated; however it remains an important and useful reference guide for scholars, despite its dry and ponderous writing style. His *History of the Persian Empire* (Chicago: University of Chicago Press, 1948, 1959, 1984) is equally authoritative, less dated, but unfortunately no less ponderous.

A. Leo Oppenheim, *Ancient Mesopotamia: Portrait of a Dead Civilization.* Chicago: University of Chicago Press, 1977. A highly detailed, well-written, and informative discussion of Mesopotamian culture by one of the recognized masters in the field.

Andre Parrot, *Arts of Assyria.* New York: Golden Press, 1961. A lavishly illustrated presentation of the works of Assyrian artists. One of the best of its kind.

Julian Reade, *Mesopotamia.* Cambridge: Harvard University Press, 1991. A short but highly informative sketch of ancient Mesopotamian culture, with many fine photos and illustrations.

Georges Roux, *Ancient Iraq.* New York: Penguin, 1980. An extremely comprehensive and well-written overview of Mesopotamian history and culture, from the prehistoric period, through the rise and fall of the major peoples who dominated the region—the Sumerians, Babylonians, Assyrians, Persians, Hellenistic Greeks, and Parthians. Highly recommended for serious students of the subject.

H. W. F. Saggs, *Civilization Before Greece and Rome*. New Haven: Yale University Press, 1989. One of the best recent books summarizing early Near Eastern cultures.

Daniel C. Snell, *Life in the Ancient Near East, 3100–332 B.C.* New Haven: Yale University Press, 1997. This sweeping overview of Near Eastern culture, customs, and ideas by Professor Snell, of the University of Oklahoma, is up-to-date, briskly written, informative, and copiously documented. Highly recommended.

Additional Works Consulted:

Maria E. Aubert, *The Phoenicians and the West*. Trans. Mary Turton. New York: Columbia University Press, 1993.

Paul G. Bahn, ed., *The Cambridge Illustrated History of Archaeology*. New York: Cambridge University Press, 1996.

Nels M. Bailkey, ed., *Readings in Ancient History: From Gilgamesh to Diocletian*. Lexington, MA: D. C. Heath, 1976.

James Henry Breasted, *Ancient Times: A History of the Early World*. Boston: Ginn and Company, 1944.

C. W. Ceram, *Gods, Graves, and Scholars: The Story of Archaeology*. Trans. E. B. Garside and Sophie Wilkins. New York: Random House, 1986.

Peter Clayton and Martin Price, *The Seven Wonders of the Ancient World*. New York: Barnes and Noble, 1993.

L. Sprague de Camp, *The Ancient Engineers*. New York: Ballantine Books, 1963.

L. Delaporte, *Mesopotamia: The Babylonian and Assyrian Civilization*. Trans. V. Gordon Childe. New York: Barnes and Noble, 1970.

Robert Drews, *The Coming of the Greeks: Indo-European Conquests in the Aegean and the Near East*. Princeton: Princeton University Press, 1988.

———, *The End of the Bronze Age: Changes in Warfare and the Catastrophe ca. 1200 B.C.* Princeton: Princeton University Press, 1993.

Henri Frankfort, *Art and Architecture of the Ancient Orient*. New York: Penguin, 1971.

Michael Grant, *The Visible Past*. New York: Scribner's, 1990.

A. Kirk Grayson, *Assyrian Rulers of the Third and Second Millennia B.C.* Toronto: University of Toronto Press, 1987.

Roberta L. Harris, *The World of the Bible*. London: Thames and Hudson, 1995.

Herodotus, *The Histories*. Trans. Aubrey de Sélincourt. New York: Penguin, 1972.

Morris Jastrow, *The Civilizations of Babylonia and Assyria*. Philadelphia: J. B. Lippincott, 1915.

Tom B. Jones, ed., *The Sumerian Problem*. New York: John Wiley, 1969.

John Keegan, *A History of Warfare*. New York: Random House, 1993.

Samuel N. Kramer, *Cradle of Civilization*. New York: Time-Life, 1967.

Seton Lloyd, *Foundations in the Dust*. New York: Thames and Hudson, 1981.

James Mellaart, *Earliest Civilizations of the Near East*. New York: McGraw-Hill, 1965.

J. N. Postgate, *Early Mesopotamia: Society and Economy at the Dawn of History*. New York: Routledge, 1992.

James B. Pritchard, ed., *Ancient Near Eastern Texts Relating to the Old Testament*. Princeton: Princeton University Press, 1969.

John M. Russell, *Sennacherib's Palace Without Rival at Nineveh*. Chicago: University of Chicago Press, 1991.

William Ryan and Walter Pitman, *Noah's Flood: The New Scientific Discoveries About the Event That Changed History*. New York: Simon & Schuster, 1998.

Chester G. Starr, *A History of the Ancient World*. New York: Oxford University Press, 1991.

Wolfram von Soden, *The Ancient Orient: An Introduction to the Study of the Ancient Near East*. Trans. Donald G. Schley. Grand Rapids: William B. Eerdmans, 1994.

Michael Wood, *Legacy: The Search for Ancient Cultures*. New York: Sterling Publishing, 1992.

Charles Leonard Woolley, *The Sumerians*. New York: Norton, 1965.

INDEX

PICTURE CREDITS

ABOUT THE AUTHOR

Historian Don Nardo has published many books about the ancient world. These include general histories, such as *The Persian Empire* and *The Decline and Fall of the Roman Empire*; war chronicles, such as *The Punic Wars* and *The Battle of Marathon*; cultural studies, such as *Life in Ancient Athens*, *Greek and Roman Sport*, *Life as a Roman Slave*, and *The Trial of Socrates*; and literary companions to the works of Homer and Sophocles. Mr. Nardo is also the editor of Greenhaven Press's *Complete History of Ancient Greece*. He lives with his lovely wife, Christine, and dog, Bud, in Massachusetts.